THE BRONCLE

A curious tale of Adoption and Reunion

Brian Bailie

ISBN: 978-1-4566-0578-0

Dedicated to my sister, Hilary
without whose curiosity so many would have remained in
ignorant bliss

And in memory of my storyteller, Philip

Contents

ACKNOWLEDGMENTS

First up, I acknowledge that there's no such thing as a normal family; mine is just one of a million tales that could be told.

I acknowledge that I shall never know or understand the whole truth behind my story of conception and adoption, either because it is now impossible to ask someone who was present at that time, or because this personal information has been withheld from me, for whatever reason.

I have attempted to be reasonable in my assumptions of character, and I now apologise if I have inadvertently caused upset or offence to the memory of anyone mentioned.

This is the story of my journey, through understanding.

THE LETTER

2nd August 2010

Dear children of Laura,

I once rode an angry bull; not intentionally – the bugger was trying to kill me. But that enlivening experience helped me realise the importance of grabbing the proverbial horns (or as it was in my case, the ears). And much as my life would be far simpler were I not to write this letter, I think I'd regret not writing it more than I might regret writing it. (I think.)

Anyhow, there's some information that I believe you deserve to know.

It was a complete coincidence that I found out about your mother's death earlier this year. I'd been searching in vain for a friend's name on Google. I entered the name of another friend, but still no results. Frustrated, I just picked a random name, and typed, 'laura adair isle of man,' and just hit the return key expecting another failed result.

I was dumbstruck. My search delivered a result on an obituary webpage.

You can call this a coincidence.

Or you can explain this as fate.

I'm not superstitious, but do things like this *really* just happen by accident?

Why did I type in your mother's name?

It *was* a name that I'd chosen at random. But it *is* a name I'm very familiar with.

Okay, here goes: There are gaps in what I know about your mother, so I'll just try and give you the facts as far as I know.

(Are you sitting comfortably?)

(I recommend it.)

I understand that your mother was separated from her husband.

I understand that as a result of this, she and her six children moved to live with her in-laws.

I understand that her mother-in-law was disabled.

You should remember the winter of 1962-'63 because it was the worst winter in Ireland for more than 200 years. Entire towns were cut off for weeks by huge snowdrifts and driving blizzards. And it was probably worse near the Mourne Mountains, causing huge snowdrifts and electricity blackouts in little towns like Newcastle, where you were living at that time.

There's just no easy way of saying this, so I'll just tell it like it is: That winter your mother conceived a child. With her father-in-law.

The pregnancy was kept a secret. And in September she gave birth to a son.

I don't know how many people knew about the child. But I know that your mother didn't want you to know. *Understandably.*

Two years later your mother gave birth to a daughter, again by her father-in-law.

The original birth certificate for the son gives your mother's full name as the mother, and an address in Newcastle. The father's name is left blank.

The original birth certificate for the daughter gives your mother's full name as the mother, and an address in Belfast. Again, the father's name is left blank.

About fifteen years ago this daughter managed to get in touch with her mother (*your* mother) through Social Services in Belfast. It was Social Services who explained your mother's circumstances to the daughter.

The daughter never made mention of the circumstances of her birth to your mother; that wasn't important to her. She naturally just wanted to make contact with her natural mother.

Your mother replied with several letters about her family, and even sent a few family photographs. But after a little while she began to back off, she was slow to reply, and her letters became very brief and impersonal.

The daughter sensed that your mother had become uncomfortable, maybe fearing that her adult children might discover her secret. So the daughter asked her if she would prefer to break contact. And your mother readily agreed.

So out of respect for your mother's secret, the daughter very reluctantly broke off all contact. Forever.

If your mother succeeded in keeping this a secret from you, then you'll be gob-smacked and very reluctant to believe me. I expect you to be sceptical, but these are the facts as they were explained to me, and confirmed by your mother's letters to the daughter.

I hope you're not angry with me for telling you this. And I hope you're not angry with your mother. Please don't be angry with your mother. It is what it is. None of us know the underlying circumstances, and none of us should judge her, or her father-in-law.

I guess you're confused about your relationship with the son and the daughter. They are your half-brother and half-sister. But because their father is *your* father's father, they are much closer than half-siblings; genetically they might be more than three-quarter siblings.

And your father (and any siblings he might have had) will also be the son and daughter's half-siblings: which also makes them your half-uncle and half-aunt.

Quite a mix up.

But what isn't a mix up is what happened to the baby daughter. She was adopted by the same parents who had adopted the son. They grew up together very happily as natural brother and sister.

There'll be lot of questions that'll remain unanswered because of your mother's death.

And out of respect for your mother, perhaps these questions should remain unasked.

It is what it is.

So, I bet you're wondering who these relative strangers are ?

On 11th September 1963 Laura gave birth to me.

And on 8th August 1965 Laura gave birth to my inquisitive sister.

Laura gave us names that may be significant in your family tree: James, and Emily. Our adopted names are Brian and Hilary.

Right now I'm feeling kind of awkward, like I've opened a can of worms and just tossed them over a stranger.

I guess you feel like you've just had a can of worms thrown at you.

Running away from a difficult situation isn't in my nature. Life happens; sometimes you just have to grab the bull by the horns. But I'm sorry if I've shocked you.

This must have been a difficult letter to read. It's been a very difficult letter to write.

I've told you just about everything I know. And although Hilary and I should have more questions to ask you than you have questions to ask us, I'll not be in contact again unless you ask me.

Yours truly,

THE CIRCUMSTANCES

Mum and Dad never had kids of their own. They'd been married about six years when a young mother offered them her baby for adoption. That was 1960, and he is my big brother, Paul. I know more about Paul's background than he does, (because when Mum began to go potty with Alzheimer's she'd just say things that she should've kept to herself; she even introduced my sister to Paul's uncle one afternoon). It's awkward because it's really none of my business, and Paul doesn't want to know, (*and realising what I've discovered in my story of adoption and reunion he might decide to just let sleeping dogs lie*).

I was adopted three years after Paul; I guess Mum and Dad wanted another kid to keep Paul company.

Being adopted is no big deal if you're adopted in infancy as I was. It's normal. It's the only world I know.

Our neighbours had three kids: twin boys, and a girl.

I reckoned that Mum decided to adopt another boy because she liked the idea of having twins. The twins next-door were great buddies who played rough and tumble together, and looked so cute dressed identically. But it didn't work so well for Paul and me. The three-year age gap didn't really help with the twin look; it never achieved the same effect. We were more like Kennedy and Khrushchev than Tweedledum and Tweedledee.

Sure, we wore the same clothes, but Paul was tall and skinny with dark eyes and straight dark hair; and I was short and fat with blue eyes and mad curly-whirly platinum-blonde hair. And we were never great buddies: rough and tumble meant beating me into submission or screwing Chinese burns on my neck; and playing football was just an excuse to kick a big wet leather ball at my face. It's fair to say that we hated each other. And this was normal too.

People adopt children for lots of reasons.

I think the most common reason is because it's a natural human instinct to be a parent.

A certain relation (who shall remain nameless for the sake of family harmony) callously remarked that Mum and Dad adopted us because we were *"the essential accessories for a respectable middle-class family."* Accessories? Like a big car? What a nasty thing to say about my mum and dad.

Okay, so being adopted is the only life I know; but *having* adopted kids was the only way Mum and Dad ever knew, and they loved us wholeheartedly and unconditionally. And looking around and listening to my friends talk about their childhood, I'd say that I was given a heap more love and affection than most *natural* offspring.

If Mum and Dad *wanted* to adopt children, they'd have done the normal thing and applied to an adoption agency; but they never did that, because we three were *offered* to them.

Furthermore, I was given two forenames that meant a lot to Mum and Dad. My first name is Thomas, and this is Dad's father's name (it's one of those family names that alternates with each generation, William, Thomas, William, Thomas, and has done for at least 250 years); and my second name, Brian, is the name of Mum's favourite uncle. I'm a full family member; I was adopted wholeheartedly, for keeps.

Two years after I was adopted, Mum and Dad adopted my sister, and she is also my full birth-sister, (and she's the reason why I found out about my birth-family).

Paul has always been forward-looking and ambitious. He faces forward on the train: he sees where he's going, not where he's been. He's never been interested in his birth-family or the circumstances of his adoption. I think he's got a really healthy attitude towards his adoption: just forget about it; it's history. He's moved on, emigrated with his career, and never looked back. He's now a naturalised Bermudian. And just as we once hated each other in equal measure, we also love each other, as true brothers should, (and I'm not just saying that to get another cheap holiday in Bermuda), *(or am I?)*.

Being female, my sister naturally sees things differently. When Hilary's body began to change with all the baby-making abilities and hormonal things that go on in a maturing young woman, she began to get really confused about how a mother could give away a helpless little baby that is created and grown in her belly for nine months. I just thought Hilary was getting a bit over-emotional about the whole thing, (you know the way girls are sometimes), but maybe it's the girls who have it sorted? Boys (especially the stoic Ulster-Scots variety, it seems) are quite good at detaching themselves from emotions like that.

When I unexpectedly saw my birth-mother's obituary, it was one of those gob-smacking moments of stunned surprise where you need to remind yourself to keep breathing, like scratching off the final winning number on a lottery card, (*that'll be the day*).

I really wasn't searching for online content about my birth-mother. I'd just been searching for the contact details of a couple of relatively well-known businesspeople, and I couldn't find any mention of them, anywhere. The last thing I expected was a top-of-the-page result for a 78 year-old woman, living (or recently deceased) on the Isle of Man. It was just one of those end-of-afternoon things bored people do.

I stared at my screen in total disbelief, reading it over and over word by word. Dumbstruck....

My first reaction was to tell Hilary. I reached for my mobile phone to send her a text message, but you can't text a thing like that? So I phoned her mobile number instead.

I should've known not to call her mobile number after the last time I had bad news to deliver. When our uncle unexpectedly died, my first reaction was to call his sister's mobile phone. She was stuck in downtown traffic in the rain; it wasn't the time or place, and I felt like a complete rat, realising that my aunt was extremely distressed and couldn't break from what she was doing, trapped and in distress. (I'm still very sorry about that.)

I imagine the ideal setting for telling a loved-one that someone special has died might be an isolated park bench overlooking a calm ocean sunset, tissues in one hand and glass of port in the other. But when I phoned Hilary she was at the check-out at Lidl's. I could hear the shop assistant beeping barcodes in the background. I'd misjudged the moment, again. I said that I'd something important to tell her, but now wasn't a good time; however I was on the edge of my seat and just absolutely *bursting* to tell her, so it didn't take much curious persuasion for me to fumble out the earth-shattering news that the woman who had given us life had died.

Lidl's hasn't been the same for Hilary since then. She now associates bargain packs of Greek dog food with bad news (and so does her dog). But like many things in life, is there ever a right way? (Actually, there is; and mobile phone is the *wrong* way.)

Hilary and I agreed to send our condolences incognito to our birth-mother's family; and in our card I asked if I could write to the family again later in the year, and asked what address I should use.

I remember when Dad died, Mum received hundreds of letters and cards from people. This grieving family could've been equally inundated with sympathy mail, and *my* card, from an Irish unknown, could have justifiably been set aside and never even read. And that would've been the end of that. But I did get a reply. And my future correspondence was welcomed.

Was 2nd August a good time to send my letter to this *other* family?

It had been five months since I'd seen that online obituary and mailed our condolences incognito. And I was going to wait another month to round it off to a respectable six (so I didn't appear to be carpetbagging), but 2nd August is a special day. It's Mum's birthday. I said to Hilary that sending the letter on Mum's birthday makes her a small part of it all (that, and the fact that *any* excuse would do to send my letter sooner than later, because we were both struggling with impatience).

Being adopted is knowing that you belong to two families:

* You've got loyal and emotional ties to one family;
* And undeniable blood-ties to another.

In a way, getting in touch with my other family could be seen as turning my back on my adopted family. And I can understand that. I can see how it might look to the extended Bailie family. But I've never thought of myself as anything other than a Bailie. Sure, I've experienced a couple of awkward moments when a family friend or relation has made a comment about me that they should've kept to themselves. I've been called a bastard a few times with more emphasis on malice than humour; but a remark that cut me to the bone was made when Hilary and I were favoured in a family will, and an elder relation exclaimed, "But you're not even blood relations." I don't think it was said in a mean-hearted way, maybe the person just saw the biological practicalities of the relationship and the words just slipped out, (or maybe they were genuinely angry and prejudiced). In any case it doesn't matter (and we evened out the bequests anyway, to avoid any ill will).

I didn't have anything to do with my conception; I didn't have any choice about which family adopted me. Everything about my conception, birth and adoption was completely out of my control. So why would people harbour any prejudice against me, (or call me a *social accessory*); shouldn't it be my birth-parents who carry the stigma?

It's a shame, because to me my adopted family is my *real* family. It's my birth-family that I feel alienated from.

It would've been so easy <u>not</u> to write that letter.

I wondered if their mother (my birth-mother) would've been angry that her secret had been exposed. Out of respect for her, I guess I should have just shrugged off her death and forgotten about it all. And kept her death a secret from Hilary. But I don't like secrets, (when people say they want to share a secret with me, I reply that I don't want to know; unless your asking me for some confidential advice or something, just keep that secret to yourself). Secrets are unhealthy, and rarely have happy endings. Do I feel like a snitch for exposing my birth-mother's life-long secret? Yeah, sure I do; ignorance is bliss, apparently. But a bottled-up secret can be corrosive.

My excuse for sending that letter is just that everything fell into place; all the ducks were in a row. You can call it coincidence, fate, or divine intervention.

I don't believe in luck: I believe that things happen, and it's your circumstances that make it turn out favourable or unfavourable.

I don't believe in fate: but I believe in positive thinking.

I don't *think* it was God. I know He works in mysterious ways, but *really*?

My Texan business partners say, "Shit happens." It's called Life.

The wait between sending that letter and receiving a reply made the days pass *very* slowly. I didn't know if I should expect a reply, but Hilary continued to pester me every day, twice a day, asking if anything had come in the mail from the Isle of Man.

And then I received a letter: a short, slightly incredulous, carefully worded reply that acknowledged my letter in a friendly enough manner, but asked for some proof before he shocked his siblings with my accusations.

I hadn't thought about proof. But it seemed an obvious, prudent and perfectly reasonable thing to ask for.

Hilary and I dug out copies of original birth certificates, and made photocopies. But we knew that the indisputable proof were the letters that their mother had sent to Hilary about fifteen years earlier. Hilary tore her house apart looking for them. (Any monkey with a computer can Photoshop changes to a copy of a birth certificate, but the letters to Hilary from *their* mother would be the absolutely unquestionable, undeniable proof.)

I think Hilary destroyed those letters when she had to break contact with her birth-mother. She kept the photographs, but got rid of the letters. She was really hurt when she realised that her birth-mother didn't want to communicate with her anymore, so I don't blame her if she did destroy the letters. I don't suppose she ever thought they'd come in handy.

I've got an old canoe. It's one of those homemade things, just a bunch of sticks covered in canvas, with an open top. My Claire and I, and our youngest son, Bowen, were squashed into this thing, paddling about in the sea on a lovely August Sunday afternoon. But not content to risk our lives in this antique death-trap on a shallow bay, we had taken to the notorious tidal rapids of Strangford Lough, and crossed the turbulent current where it's nearly 200 feet deep to make a dash for the placid waters of Castleward Bay on the other side.

It was a cracker day, and there's nowhere like it. We broke out our picnic on the isolated headland facing Audley's Castle, and relaxed into the thick springy tufts of sea pink and couch grass to eat our lunch. It was a perfectly warm and peaceful, beautiful summer's day.

Claire lay down with her nose in another novel while Bowen and I slipped back into the canoe and glided effortlessly into the honey-still waters of the bay to hunt for jellyfish. And then my phone rang. (I know what you're thinking, it used to be that you'd go places like this to get away from distractions like telephones, but my mobile phone sealed in a freezer-bag would be indispensable if that old canoe finally collapsed on us.)

Hilary was phoning me. And she was so excited she could hardy get the words out. She'd had a phone call, from *one of them*.

I'd never heard Hilary so animated and exhilarated.

"They phoned. Our *other* brother, Graham phoned. And the first thing he said to me was, *Welcome*." She was almost crying with joy. I think she'd given up any hope of contact fifteen years ago when she broke contact with our birth-mother, and she'd been trying so hard to subdue any real hope of a reply to my letter to avoid another anticlimax. So all of a sudden she'd kind of, popped.

"You've got to phone him."

"I'm in a canoe, on Strangford Lough."

"You've got to phone him. I told him you would."

"uuuh,................ okay." I wet my finger and wrote his number on the warm canvas body of the canoe.

"It's starting to dry and disappear. Got to hang up before it's gone. I'll call you back."

A beautiful brown and orange Lion's Mane jellyfish pulsated below us in slow motion, too big for Bowen's net. If I was to make this potentially life-changing phone call anywhere, sure wasn't this just the perfect place to do it.

I keyed in the numbers, checked them carefully against the salty numbers fading on the canoe, and I cautiously pressed the 'Call' button.

I watched the display, waiting for it to tell me when I was connected.

What was I going to say? What *was* I going to say? What the blue bloody blazes am I doing?

'Connected' Dang.

What *was* I doing? And why *was* I doing it? I still haven't really figured *that* out.

Why did I send the letter? I think I did it for Hilary. Sure I'm curious, but I think it's because Hilary believes she *needs* a connection to this other reality. Is that putting it too strong? (Maybe not strong enough.) She says it's because they're our natural birth-family, as if it's our right, and their right to know. I dunno; but at that moment in time it didn't feel right, or very natural.

I've always been very comfortable as a Bailie. And I've no intention of switching family loyalties, or adopting new ones. (Oh, that's an odd thought: Adopting my birth-family.) I am Brian Bailie. I was an *Adair* for maybe the first nine months of my existence in some Belfast hospital nursery, or wherever (I don't remember any of it). I may be their half-brother-half-uncle. But I'm not one of *them*, and I don't yet know if I'll ever want to be. Of course I'm related by blood, (almost full-strength), but I feel like they're foreigners.

Being adopted is just like being married. It's a legally binding arrangement where a person becomes a full member of another family, in name, in loyalty, inheritance and everything. You never hear about an adopted person getting divorced from their family. It works. It's an ancient accepted way of family life that even makes the headlines in the Bible, (notably Moses, and Jesus). So I'm in pretty good company.

Drifting in the serene silky peacefulness of Castleward Bay, my heart was pounding like I'd just been wrestling that damned bull again. "Hello. Graham? Brian here. Hilary's brother."

His soft voice replied, "Welcome." same as he'd begun with Hilary.

Welcome.

Thinking back, at the time that word was a good choice; it was nice and familiar and welcoming. But thinking about it now, it makes me feel like a long-lost relation returning to the family, seeking acceptance. That's definitely not what I was after. I'm no prodigal son. I'm not returning; exploring, perhaps.

We chatted easily, like old friends.

It was surreal.

There was a strange and immediate familiarity, a true connection.

To be sure, Graham did most of the talking. He spoke about growing up near the Mournes, moving to

Newcastle, boarding schools, and moving to the Isle of Man, and aunts and uncles, and his mother and father, and his grandfather.

Strange, because although he was talking about places and people significant to my very existence, it meant very little to me at the time; my mind was focussed on the significance of the phone call, not its content. It was like listening to a stranger talk about their life. (I get that a lot. Either I look like I'm interested, look like I can help, or look like I've got *sucker* written across my head. Or perhaps it's because I'm a listener, and everyone wants someone to listen.)

Graham was phoning me from his home in Bournemouth. He was the only surviving sibling not living on the Isle of Man. Ewan (his brother whom I'd sent my letter to) presumably couldn't contain himself long enough to wait for Hilary's missing correspondence with their mother, and had shown my letter to his brother and sisters on the island, and then read it over the phone to Graham.

I'd put my full name on the letter, and my full address, so it didn't take a lot of investigation to find my phone number, or Hilary's. But Graham was the one who grasped the nettle and phoned. He'd tried me first (but I was out, paddling about), so without hesitation he'd phoned Hilary. Why wait, I suppose?

There was just one question I needed to ask.

I've always had a fear that my birth-mother was dominated by her father-in-law. I wanted them to be lovers; I wanted to be the unexpected result of a loving respect for each other. I knew I was a mistake, but I didn't want to be the consequence of abuse. That would trouble me. It would trouble me to think that the man who fathered me was cruel and had forced his vulnerable and desperate daughter-in-law to have sex.

Graham assured me that the relationship between his mother and grandfather was a very special one, a loving and caring and respectful relationship. And he went on to say that my letter had made sense of a lot of things for him.

Graham spoke until my phone battery died. I paddled back across the bay to find Claire and tell her what had just happened.

My Claire reads too many novels, sometimes two a week, sometimes one a day if it's particularly gruesome. Now she was witnessing a real-life drama, so she was wide-eyed and buzzing with excitement when I told her who I'd been talking to on the phone. Of course, she wanted to know everything. And of course (being a man), I could only remember enough of the conversation to make her livid with curiosity, and irritated that I could be *so* vague about something *so* dramatic. But Graham's conversation just seemed unreal to me, like I was having a daydream. And he'd talked so long and told me so much that I couldn't sort it all out in my head to tell Claire anything other than snippets and headlines. I said I'd phone Hilary when we got home, she'd remember, Hilary would've taken notes.

The tide was now running fast and full outside the safety of the bay. We'd have to cross a lot of turbulence to get back to the peninsula side of the lough. And once we'd started across the narrows I realised I hadn't planned our route very well. We were well away from the whirlpool (that beastie would've swallowed us up and spat us out in bits), but I didn't realise how fast the tide was shifting until we were deep into 9-knots of boiling water. We paddled through great bulges of smooth turbulence where the water is forced up by underwater rock formations, and our little canoe spun this way and that like a crazy compass needle, nearly tipping us out time and again.

"Just keep low and paddle hard. Don't try to correct our course. *Just keep paddling.*"

Bowen was enjoying the ride. Claire was scared, but she remained calm so as not to panic Bowen. I'd have enjoyed it if I was on my own, but I knew that Claire was going to give me a serious case of earache and a paddle-shaped face if we all ended up swimming for it.

There was no going back on the course of events I'd started by sending that letter. Whether I was riding an angry bull, riding the tidal rapids, or writing to my birth-family, I knew there was no going back. I'd started something I was going to have to see through, and whatever they might be, I was going to have to live with the consequences.

THE BACKGROUND

After Graham had broken the ice with his impulsive phone call, his siblings began to get in touch by phone, letters and emails. And there was a flurry of new friend activity on Facebook from their extended families. There seemed to be a lot of them. It was daunting. What *had* I started?

I know I'd shocked them all with the proof that their mother had produced a couple of extra children, but the real gob-smacker for them was that *my* father was *their* father's father.

My birth certificate proved that their mother, Laura, was my birth-mother. But I'd no evidence that their grandfather had fathered me: only the word of a retired social worker, and the missing letters their mother had sent to Hilary over fifteen years ago.

I'd caused a lot of upset. I'd caused a lot of astonishment. I know, because they told me so.

What had I hoped to achieve by exposing their mother's secret? I still don't know; perhaps, like I said, everything just fell into place. Did they deserve to know; did they *need* to know; should I have exposed their mother's secret? Probably not.

When Hilary had written to Social Services all those years ago, she needed answers:

- She needed to know who she was.
- She needed to know where she was from.
- She needed to know why she'd been given up for adoption.
- She needed to identify herself.
- And let's face it, everyone loves to investigate a secret, (especially if you're the secret).

Mum and Dad accepted Hilary's curiosity, and they both supported her wholeheartedly. Mum said that she'd always expected that we'd want to know more about where we came from, who we were, and why we'd been offered for adoption.

I'd always known that Hilary was my full sister. Apart from the fact that we look like natural siblings, Mum had always told us so. As a little girl, Hilary always said she wanted to be a farmer's wife when she grew up, (I couldn't decide what I wanted to be, and I'm still waiting to grow up), so when the social worker told Hilary that her birth-family had a farm, she was delighted and said she felt an instinctive urge to wear dungarees and feed chickens.

Discovering your identity is usually fairly easy for an adopted person.

After about a year of putting it off, Hilary's persistence won me over and I made the time to visit the General Register's Office.

I like Belfast; it's a droll city that has in some ways benefitted from thirty years of bombing and rebuilding. Unfortunately no terrorist had the foresight to remodel the hideously unremarkable building that houses the General Register's Office. I entered the unwelcoming block of glass and steel on Chichester Street, and woke the nice woman slouched behind the bulletproof window to ask her what I had to do to see my birth certificate. It was simple: she just needed my name, my address, and a Five Pound note. Then she told me to go away again; I'd receive a Certified Copy of Original Birth Certificate in about a week by mail.

I'd almost forgotten about the impending arrival of the certificate by the time it arrived in the post. I eagerly ripped it open, anticipating some marvellous revelation.

I was so disappointed, *so* disheartened.

My mother had named me '*Eric James* Adair,' and I hated it like a bad joke, like someone had written *kick my arse* on my back; like everyone would laugh (and did laugh) when I'd eventually tell them (*many* years later).

I've never really felt like I owned my adopted names, *Thomas*, and *Brian*; not because I knew I was adopted, ... it's just that they never felt like a good fit for my personality.

My first name, Dad's father's name, is Thomas. A good solid-sounding name, and my grandfather was someone I really admired, (although he died six years before I was born, he'd been a successful entrepreneur and politician and reformer, and everyone who had known him only ever had good things to say about him). My middle name, Mum's favourite uncle's name, is Brian. Uncle Brian was a doctor in Comber, and he was also a very popular and well-respected man; *everyone* loved Dr Brian Henry.

But despite owning two precious family names, I still don't feel like a Brian, or a Tom or Tommy or Thomas. I don't know what name would suit me. I ask my Claire what she thinks, and (guess what) she says I look like a Brian, (she's obviously still blinded by infatuation).

You know the way most people look like their name? Well, personally that never worked for me, I think. And then I finally discover the names my birth-mother chose for me, and I'm so disappointed. Eric James? Eric Adair sounds like a geeky technical manager, thin hair and thick glasses (no offence intended to balding, bespectacled technicians), but it's just not me. James, Jim, Jimmy; that's not me either. I've never felt like an Eric or a James (and I don't feel like an Adair, either). (Pillow talk with my Claire, I asked her if I looked like a Jim Adair: *that* woke her up, laughing.)

If you had to pick your own name, what would *you* choose? Chances are that you're happy with what you've got. I don't think mine is a problem with being adopted, or with adopting another family's choice of names for me. My brother has a great name: 'Paul' is such a clean sounding, honest and reliable name; 'Brian' sounds like a henchman.

Names are important to me. When our kids were born, Claire and I took a long time to consider good names for each of them. Claire wanted to call our first boy Brian, but (yes, you guessed it) I wouldn't have it; so we sort of way named him after her, and he's called Blair. Then we had a daughter, and I agreed to do the same sort of thing and we named her after me, and she's called Briar. Then, when we found out that our third child was going to be a boy we had a couple of months to think of a name. I wanted to give him a manly yet gentle-sounding Celtic name, and we eventually chose to name him Bowen.

Our kids tell us that they love their names, and sure enough they all look like their names suit their personalities. But *I* don't feel like I suit Thomas or Brian, or Eric or James. At school I was called Bailie, which would've been okay had it been pronounced "Bay-Lee", however a typical Ulster accent pronounces the name more like, "Bee-Alee", and I didn't like that either.

I was *so* disappointed when I saw what my birth-mother had chosen for me; perhaps she knew it didn't matter because my names would be changed anyway. I don't know what I was hoping for, I've yet to hear a name that I'd like to go by. (I know what you're thinking, stop moaning about it – it's just a name.)

Our birth-mother had named Hilary, 'Emily'. Hilary likes that name, and she prefers it to Hilary.

Hilary had been corresponding with our birth-mother through a social worker since 1993. She had shown me the letters from our birth-mother, and the photographs. The letters were short generalised chit-chat, but the photographs spoke a thousand words and fascinated us the most, and we examined every detail of every face for a similarity to ourselves, (no harm to them, but they *did* look like a bit of an odd bunch).

Sure, I'd like to have written to my birth-mother too, but the correspondence seemed so slow and complicated. Making direct contact between adopted children and estranged birth-parents wasn't considered a good idea for lots of sensible reasons, so everything went through this social worker who, I guess, censored our correspondence before forwarding the mail in a brown envelope to our mother. And it worked the same way in reverse. It seemed so unnecessarily nosey and slow and inconvenient. (And what would I write, anyway? *"Hi, how are you? It's been a while,......"*)

Although we only had a nutshell synopsis of the circumstances surrounding our origins, Hilary and I had had a long time to accept what the social worker had told us about our natural parents, and I kind of liked it: it's fun to realise that I've a father sixty years my senior, (the old scallywag).

But for my birth-mother's family, receiving my letter five months after their mother's death must've been a really shocking revelation that turned their whole world upside-down. My letter interrupted the lives of this blissfully ignorant family, and shocked them with a story that contradicted the established memories they enjoyed of their recently departed mother, and their grandfather.

Slowly, (more slowly for some than others), the rest of their family began to accept the facts.

They had enjoyed one unshakable memory of their mother; they thought that they had known her and understood her personality, and I'd shattered all that in the time it took to read half my letter. They'd never even suspected that their mother held a secret, and certainly not a secret like me, nor another like Hilary.

They had adored and respected their mother. And they had worshiped their grandfather. How had I affected their memories and ingrained opinions of such very special people to them?

THE PREFIX

Identifying my birth-parents within this story is important to me, because I don't want to imply any disrespect to the parents who adopted me and raised me and loved me and called me their own.

But adding the *birth-* prefix every time that I mention my birth-parents is tiresome to continue reading. So from here on, patient reader, the parents who adopted me, (the *Bailie's*), are identified as my mum and dad. And the parents who fortuitously created me, (*Laura* and her father-in-law, *Billy*), are identified as my mother and father. I'm dropping the *birth-* prefix.

And on this point, (having been adopted), (and having been foster-father to eight children), I think I'm qualified to reinforce the point that being a mother or a father is a world apart from being a mum or a dad.

Most reasonably healthy people have the ability, *the gift*, to reproduce another human being and become a mother or a father. But being a mum or a dad is something much, much more special.

As a foster-father, I've seen the effects of poor parenting; I've had to work very hard to help the children of loveless, abusive, and neglectful parents. It takes a whole bunch of unconditional love and a heap of patience to readjust a child, to undo enough of the emotional damage so that they have a reasonable chance of realising their full potential.

There is a world of difference between the ability to be a parent, and the talent to be a *good* parent; there's a *world* of difference between a father and a dad; a *world* of difference between a mother, and a mum. If I sound annoyed it's not because I feel that I need to differentiate between my father and mother, and my dad and mum; I'm just upset when I think of some of the abuse that my foster-children suffered at the hand of their own parents. I'm sure that offering me for adoption was a very difficult decision for my parents to make; but it *was* a decision made in my best interests.

THE WINGER

My newfound *other* family began to send me photographs and anecdotes and snippets of information from here, there and everywhere. Obviously they knew a lot about their mother, but my natural instinct drove me to discover more about my father, their grandfather.

None of what they told me about my father made much sense, separately. So I pulled together all the letters and emails and photographs to try to put the life of this man into some sort of chronological sense, to place his story into the historical context of the times and places he had lived. The snippets and anecdotes I'd been offered left too many unanswered questions.

Billy Adair was my father.

He was the father-in-law to my mother, Laura; and the grandfather to my mother's surviving children.

He was born in 1903, the youngest of thirteen children to a farming family in the townland of Ballylough, near the smart little town of Castlewellan that nestles in the peaceful foothills of the Mourne Mountains. His father (my grandfather), Robert Adair, was born in 1845 (the year in which the Great Famine began in Ireland); he was married in 1880 to Agnes, who gave birth to Billy when she was 42 years old.

That's a big generation gap between Robert and Billy and me.

Fifty-eight years separate Robert and Billy

Sixty years separate Billy and me. Why it's like Old Testament generation gaps: my grandfather is 118 years my senior.

Now that I think of it, my Claire's family is the complete opposite. Claire is sixteen years younger than her mother, and her mother is seventeen years younger than her grandmother. So my natural grandfather would've been 91 when my Claire's grandmother was born.

I wonder how my Claire would react if I tried to maintain my family tradition, and I did a little procreation when I'm about 60 years old? (Actually, I've a pretty good idea how she'd react, and it'd probably involve a mallet and a pair of pliers.)

I like the idea of having a link to the Mourne Mountains. The mountains aren't especially big, but they are impressively beautiful and uplifting; the motherly undulations of their outline overlook the Irish Sea and surrounding counties for miles and miles. Gently resting at the edge of the Irish Sea, they must be one of the most beautiful natural features in the whole of Ireland.

I've cycled past the little townland Ballylough more often than I've driven past it, and yet I can't say that I've ever really noticed the place. It's off to the right, just next Annsborough, near the bottom of that hill from Clough, before the road rises again into that slow agonising ascent to Castlewellan.

Ballylough isn't a settlement, it's just another townland of lush green lumpy fields with big stone walls and overgrown hedges, it's most significant feature is the decent sized fishing lake near the brow of the hill. And it's usually raining. It could be anywhere in rural Ireland. All the same, the place is beautiful and very peaceful under the close gaze of the Mournes.

I worked as a farm worker for a while.

I loved to soak up my surroundings: notice the grasses and brightly coloured weeds dancing in the breeze; recognise the scent of the earth in each field, and the scent of each changing season; I enjoyed watching the different kinds of wildlife all around me; on a clear summer's day I'd stand and strain my eyes into the blue to find the skylark singing his song high above my head. I loved farming; I loved the labour and the lifestyle; it felt right to me, like a well-worn pair of wellyboots.

The land I worked was on the sea-side of the Ards Peninsula, near Ballywalter. The farmland ran down to the open sandy shore of the Irish Sea from where you can see the distant horizons of Scotland and the Isle of Man on almost any fair day.

I'd probably still be working there had it not been for something my dad said one day. He asked me what I was hoping to do with myself, meaning: when are you going to stop playing farmer, and get yourself a real job.

Dad wasn't being mean; he was being a dad to me. He was asking me when I was going to exploit my full potential and use my natural talents and intelligence to do more with my life than labouring on a farm. And, though it upset me at the time, Dad was dead right, and he made me think. I left farming about a year after that, after a stupid argument with the farm manager who was convinced that I was after his job. I regret leaving on bad terms with the man, after all it was just the two of us working the farm, and we were like brothers most of the time. But Dad was right, I'd had my fun and it was time to do something else.

I know that Billy grew up on a farm, a son of a farmer. The 1911 Census of Ireland tells me this. This makes me glad, because when I fortuitously became a farmer I really felt like I belonged to that life and that tough wholesome work, like it was in my blood.

In 1920, aged seventeen, Billy joined the Ulster Special Constabulary, locally known as the B-Specials. The B-Specials were initially just a rabble of part-time reserve policemen who were supposed to support the regular police who were struggling to control the growing threat of republican unrest.

This was the start of the Irish War of Independence. Southern parts of counties Down and Armagh were home to a very high percentage of Roman Catholics, many of whom were naturally sympathetic to the republican cause, but the ruling Unionist government couldn't afford to risk losing this region of Ireland if a north-south split divided the island, (a key reason being that Belfast risked losing control of its main source of drinking water from the Mourne Mountains).

The B-Specials were a part-time armed militia, especially trained for counter-guerrilla operations (and often described as Orangemen with guns); it didn't take long for them to earn themselves a reputation for being very heavy-handed against Roman Catholics. The B-Specials reacted brutally against republican violence; their reprisals for IRA ambushes often included the demolition of houses, shops and pubs owned by suspected republican sympathisers.

The B-Specials didn't have an official uniform until 1922. In 1920, like a true vigilante, Billy carried his guns while wearing his everyday clothes.

Armed, authorised, and high on adrenaline, the B-Specials often acted on their own initiative, like a law unto themselves in the bandit country that would soon become the border between Northern Ireland and the Irish Free State. It was a risky job; more than ninety of their fellow police officers were killed on duty between 1920 and 1922.

From Carrickmacross to Crossmaglen there are more rogues than honest men, or so the saying goes.

The border area around southern County Down and southern County Armagh is ideal guerrilla country. Lots of lonely little country roads, dense copses, dry-stone walls, gentle green hills and fertile valleys. It's very green and very beautiful, and for the most part it remains an ancient unspoilt landscape. But anytime I've travelled in the area I always felt like I was being watched. In fact I knew I was being watched: by the British Army (among others).

When I was about 18, I was minding my own business driving the road between Crossmaglen and Newtownhamilton when a single British soldier stepped into the road in front of me and pointed his rifle into my face. He just wanted to ask where I'd been and where I was going; I could've told him anything of course, but I knew that the other twenty or so in his platoon were hidden in the overgrowth and each had their rifles trained on me with safety catches off, while my name and the details of my car were checked with the police. (The joke is that I might have had just as much chance of being stopped by the Provisional IRA and asked the same questions.)

Apart from the ridiculous and intrusive hill forts that the British Army had delivered by helicopter to erect on advantageous hilltops, I don't expect that border landscape has changed in millennia. It remains perfect bandit country, and it's not a great place to try to control an international border.

The IRA in the early 1920s had become a reasonably well-organised guerrilla army intent on achieving its aim of kicking the British out of Ireland, (and not without good historical motives); however the protestant majority in Ulster had equally strong reasons for resisting.

The small isolated farms and communities on the periphery of the Ulster protestant population were most at risk of republican intimidation and persecution. And that's how it was for young Billy Adair. Joining the B-Specials meant he was given a gun and taught how to use it effectively. This helped him to protect his home from attack; but it also made him a legitimate target in a rural area where everyone knew everyone else's business.

Returning from patrol on a dark November night in 1920, the IRA ambushed Billy's unit while they passed through Newry town. One of Billy's colleagues was shot dead in the attack; Billy caught a bullet in his left arm that shattered his elbow. His left arm had to be amputated. That's how he got the nickname 'the Winger.' He had just turned seventeen years old.

Am I proud that my father was a member of the B-Specials?

No, not really. But I wasn't there, I don't know what it was like, and I'm not going to judge the man. He lived in difficult times when his way of life was threatened by the political ambitions of the Irish republican movement; and his life was at real risk simply because of his religious background.

I grew up during the recent Troubles. Bombing was normal; killings and punishment beatings were reported almost everyday. Heavily armed police and army were everywhere, patrolling the streets weighed down with armour and equipment; driving in convoy along the roads, casually pointing their rifles out the open back doors and roof of their armoured vehicles; and buzzing in the air was the constant drone of a static helicopter watching everything. It was normal. But I never felt a desire to join the police or army to protect my community.

The whole political situation was a mess (and below the surface, it still is), and I never wanted to be a politician's puppet. Even though Dad would've loved to follow his father into politics (and he was well capable of it), he knew the risks to his family were too great. (Dad knew plenty of politicians. They called at our house now and again, and they all had to carry personal weapons, many had bodyguards; and before leaving, as a matter of routine they double-checked their cars for booby-trap bombs. That's no way to live.)

In *my* opinion, the B-Specials were a bunch of bullies. But they operated in areas where they were heavily outnumbered; and in that situation, I guess, being a bully is just a survival tactic, isn't it? Like a farmer in a field full of boisterous adolescent bulls: he's going to let the beasts know who's in charge by administering an occasional disciplinary whack of a stick to an impudent nose, (though I can tell you, this tactic *can* backfire dramatically).

Billy would have received some financial compensation from the British government for losing his arm on duty; but he was a farmer, and farming wasn't a job for a one-armed man, certainly not in the 1920s.

In the 1920s the farm where I worked would've been about 140 acres with fourteen fulltime labourers. When I was there, the farm had grown to about 340 acres, and there was just me and the farm manager to work it. There were still old tools and bits of vintage equipment lying about the fields and yard buildings, so it's easy for me to understand that farming in Billy's era was a tough labour-intensive struggle of man against nature, only suitable for fit agile men; it was all horses and hobnailed boots. For Billy, losing his arm meant losing his farming heritage.

I left farming very reluctantly after only seven years; I can't imagine how broken Billy must've felt to realise that he'd never actively work a farm again.

Billy met his wife in hospital while he recovered from his amputation.

Despite all the thousands of surgical procedures performed during the First World War, amputation in 1920 was still a very risky operation that relied on the use of antiseptics to keep the wound free from infection, (it would be another eight years before Alexander Fleming discovered the penicillin antibiotic). However, antiseptics were more effective in destroying the patient's natural immune defences than effectively preventing the invading bacteria, so amputees still had a high risk of death from infection regardless of the quality of the surgery.

Billy had lost his left arm, and with the loss of his arm he lost his ability to do the work he knew. As his nurse, Muriel's job was to care for his wound, keep a check against infections, and keep his spirits up.

The old hospital at Daisy Hill in Newry was due for replacement in the 1920s. Built beside the old workhouse, it was a barracks of a place, segregated into Protestant and Roman Catholic wards; and the small nursing staff were still reeling from the flood of patients caused by the Spanish Flu epidemic just a year earlier.

I expect that Muriel's pity for the eighteen year-old loyalist hero won Billy her special attention and, as is often the way, the young nurse fell in love with her patient, and Billy gradually fell in love with his nurse. He had lost an arm, and gained a girl.

Billy and Muriel married soon after, and produced three boys and a girl: Robert, David, Daniel, and Jane. These children are my half-brothers and half-sister.

In the mid-1920s private motorcars were hand-built luxuries, unaffordable to the average person; and the railways only served key routes between industrial towns. So I guess that Billy realised an opportunity to invest his compensation money when he became a partner in a small rural bus company. He operated a little bus christened the Ulster Star. It had modern pneumatic tyres and offered a comfortable ride for up to 16 seated passengers.

In the mid-1920's anyone with a drivers and vehicle licence could operate a bus service. Bus companies competed head-to-head on the same routes, winning customers based on price, the comfort of their coaches, or how fast they could get you where you're going. Speeding and overcrowding were common offences for early bus operators. A bus conductor could charge any fair he could get away with, and operate on any route he wanted. Deals were made by bus operators to collect customers and deliver them directly to the venue that offered them the biggest back-hander, be it a grocery store, public house, football match, or cinema.

Tighter regulations for busses began to be enforced from 1926, and from 1928 busses were officially regulated by an act of parliament.

From 1928 drivers and busses still had to be licensed, but the new regulations meant that as a conductor, Billy *also* required a licence; and their bus route and schedules had to be applied for, for official approval. This worked out okay for most established bus owners because once their schedules were approved they owned the monopoly on those routes so long as they continued to provide a satisfactory service.

I guess that Billy's little bus company paid its way, but it wasn't going to make the partners wealthy without a major investment to remain competitive. Other bus operators were growing and merging, and aggressively buying up the licences for the most profitable routes. By the mid-1930s Northern Ireland Road Transport Board was effectively nationalising the bus industry, forcing takeovers on the most profitable bus routes. Billy's little bus company was eventually put out of business within Northern Ireland, and forced to scrape a living from cross-border excursions.

After his short career as a one-armed rural bus conductor, Billy enjoyed a change of fortunes.

By the end of the Second World War, Billy had bought a quarry.

Goraghwood Quarry produced the fine-grained green-grey granite that had been used for the construction of many local buildings and bridges, including the long, curved, 18-arch Craigmore Viaduct that raises the Belfast to Dublin mainline 140 feet high, over the Camlough and Bessbrook rivers, just outside of Newry town.

Goraghwood was a going concern when Billy bought it, and the granite was in big demand. This quarry supplied the ballast that supported the railway sleepers for most of the rail networks in Ireland. And as the wartime restrictions to the building industry were coming to an end, Northern Ireland was enjoying a building boom to catch up with the development of roads, and offices, schools, public buildings and homes; quality stone was in big demand.

Billy had also purchased a sizeable farm in the townland of Dromantine, near to the substantial country house where he lived at Jerrettspass, north of Newry. He moved from this house in the late-1950s to live in a villa in the popular seaside resort of Newcastle.

Billy's wife suffered a stroke a couple of years after he'd moved to live in Newcastle. That was 1960, just a year after Billy's daughter-in-law, Laura, and her six children had come to live with them. Muriel's stroke paralysed the right side of her body and she lost her ability to speak. Their roles were now reversed from when they first met forty years earlier as nurse and patient. Billy and his daughter-in-law, Laura, cared for Muriel at home, and slowly helped her learn to walk again.

Despite the pressures at home (looking after Muriel, and being father-figure to six young grandchildren), Billy bought a hotel in 1962. The Avoca Hotel still stands at the end of the promenade in Newcastle, at the foot of the tallest mountain in Ireland.

Laura helped Billy run the Avoca Hotel. And business was good. Newcastle is still a magnet for visitors, but in the early 1960s the seaside town attracted huge crowds of day-trippers and holidaymakers bussed in by the coach-load from the big smoke of Belfast, just 45 miles away to the north.

In 1968 Billy purchased another hotel.

The Conister Hotel sat slap-bang in the middle of Douglas promenade, on the Isle of Man. The hotel's name comes from the hazardous Conister Rocks in Douglas Bay. There's a Victorian folly built on those rocks that serves as a warning landmark and a refuge for stricken sailors.

I wonder if Billy saw his Conister hotel as a refuge? Yes, I *know* he did. I know for a fact that rumours were beginning to spread about his relationship with Laura; I know for a fact that rumours were beginning to spread about two children born illegitimately by their relationship. Billy fled to the Isle of Man, and he took Laura and her family with him.

Laura moved with her children to live at the Conister Hotel in 1969, and just as she had with the Avoca, she managed the hotel for her father-in-law, Billy.

Laura continued to run the Conister Hotel until 1980, when it was sold to the owners of the adjacent Empress Hotel.

Billy Adair often told his grandchildren that his business career began with a three-legged sheep that he bought for a Pound.

To achieve so much is quite an accomplishment for anyone. Billy was clearly a very determined and persistent, charming and forceful, resourceful and successful businessman. But there's another side to his character: Billy was a man who knew the importance of family.

Billy cared for his wife at home for eleven years after she suffered her stroke in 1960. He'd initially taken the doctor's advice to place Muriel in the care of a private nursing home, but she had been left to sit unstimulated for hours on end. So Billy brought her home again, angry with himself for abandoning his wife that way. With help from private nurses, Billy and Laura cared for Muriel at his house on Bryansford Road, dressing her, bathing her, feeding her, toileting her, and teaching her how to walk and communicate again.

And when Billy's aging bothers and sisters needed care, he cared for them as well. His home was *their* home; each in turn, they were nursed and kept comfortable and dignified until they died. He travelled to Canada to check on his brother Tommy, and even sent his granddaughter to live there and care for Tommy and his wife for a full year (and Billy covered all the expenses).

I know from my own experience (with Dad dying, Mum's Alzheimer's, and looking out for my disabled uncle), that putting family first isn't the easy option; it's expensive, time-consuming and stressful (isn't that why there are so many private care homes today). I don't know if I admire Billy more for his devotion to his family, or for his business success against the odds.

But I know what you're thinking: this *family comes first* policy of Billy's conflicts with giving Hilary and me away for adoption. Maybe so; but I know that Billy and Laura were in love, I'm sure it wasn't *just* sex, I'm convinced they were making love. And, to have to give away their children who had been conceived in love must have been a very difficult decision that broke their hearts.

Claire and I used to foster young children, each of whom had suffered abuse or neglect in varying extremes, in one way or another. These kids weren't our children (far from it), but in every case letting go was always very emotional and very difficult for us. We were only caring for these kids for a little while, (some for a few months, others for a few years); if Claire and I struggled with this final separation, I can't imagine how difficult it was for Billy and Laura to make the decision to give up their perfectly helpless little babies for adoption.

Would I have liked to meet Billy, my father?

Mmm, ... I *think* so. But maybe not.

Billy died when I was still ten years old, so the sixty-year age gap would've meant a major communication gap. I'd rather have met him when I was more mature.

But even if the age gap wasn't an issue, I think it would've been more difficult for him than for me. I'd like to have heard his voice and known his laugh. I'd like to recognise his gait, and watch his body language. I'd like to know what he liked, what made him laugh, and what irritated him. Yeah.... I guess I'd liked to have met him. Of course I would. But it would've been awkward. I'm not sure that he'd have wanted to meet me. Despite his strong character, I think he might've been ashamed, somehow; ashamed that he was forced to give me away.

All of Billy's children to his wife are dead now.

These people were my half-brothers and half-sister. I don't know what to think about that. In a way I feel like Hilary and I are spares.

I'd like to have met these half-siblings, but again, I don't think they'd have liked to meet me. In any case I don't think they'd have the same fond memories to share of their father that his grandchildren have of him. That's often how it is.

When I was a kid I became great friends with by my next-door neighbour, Bob Nixon. We spent a lot of time together; he was retired, and I had plenty of time on my hands having been kicked out of school at 16. Bob had been to medical school at Queens University Belfast with my namesake, Mum's favourite uncle, Brian Henry. And Bob had also known Dad's father, (Tom Bailie had been MP for North Down since 1941 until Bob defeated him at the 1953 general election). Bob taught me a lot about life. He taught me to respect even the humblest person, and to give as much care to a menial task as to an important one. I loved him like a father. But I was talking to one of Bob's sons recently, telling him how important and influential his father was in my life, and his son's reply shocked me. He told me that he'd a completely different memory of his father: a hard-hearted and demanding man, too busy to engage with his children.

Given Billy's business enterprises, and his after-hours involvement with the Freemasons and the Orange Institution, Billy probably had much the same relationship with his children as Bob had offered his. So perhaps, even if I could've, my half-siblings, Robert, David, Daniel and Jane might not have been the best people for me to ask what *our* father was like.

Laura Adair, my mother, was married to Billy's eldest son, Robert.

Laura grew up on a farm in the townland of Lurgancahone, near Rathfriland in County Down. She had been engaged to be married to Daniel Adair, another of Billy's sons, but Daniel was two-timing Laura during their engagement, and his lover became pregnant. Laura's engagement was called off, and Daniel did the decent thing and married his pregnant lover.

I expect that Laura was naturally devastated; she'd been broken-hearted and humiliated by Daniel's betrayal. I guess that as Daniel's elder brother, Robert kept in touch with Laura to make sure she was alright; and I guess they became close because of this.

Robert and Laura married in November 1950. She was 18 years old.

Did Robert take advantage of this jilted girl?

Did Laura marry Robert on the rebound from her heartbreak with Daniel?

Was it love; or was it a convenient way to remove herself from the knowing looks and tongue-wagging that goes on in small rural communities?

I find it very curious that prior to this wedding, Billy met with Laura's parents and assured them that Laura would be looked after. Billy gave his personal guarantee that he would look after his future daughter-in-law. I know I'm repeating myself, but what's going on here?

When my daughter becomes engaged to be married it'll be *me* telling her that *I'm* always going to be there for her. When my son becomes engaged, I can't imagine having to reassure his fiancée's parents that *their* daughter will be looked after. The only reason for making a personal assurance like this will be if there *is* a perceived risk, isn't it?

Okay, so his other son, Daniel, had cheated on Laura, and this must have been devastating and maddening for her family, but did her new engagement to Robert really necessitate a personal reassurance? What *was* the perceived risk? Put it like this: if my daughter became engaged to be married, and her fiancée's father came to me to offer his personal assurance that he would make sure that my daughter would be *"looked after"*, I'd be worried. It's like strapping on a parachute, and just before I leap out of the aircraft the guy who packed my main canopy takes me aside and gives his personal reassurance that the emergency parachute *will look after me*. What's going on; what does he know that I don't know?

My opinion is mixed about this. I can't decide. Billy was saying either: Robert shouldn't be judged on Daniel's actions, or; there's a potential problem with Robert, but don't worry, I'll look out for your daughter. Or is it really possible that Billy had other plans for Laura's future? Surely not.

Robert and Laura set up home in an old converted National School schoolhouse at Dromantine in the townland of Killybodagh, half way between Newry and Poyntz Pass, which was about three miles from Billy's home, Kilbodagh House at Jerrettspass. Robert kept some livestock, and worked for his father at Goraghwood Quarry.

Laura and Robert had six children in quick succession: Rob, Heather, Olivia, Graham, Ewan, and Frank.

In 1959 Laura left her husband and took her children to live with her in-laws in Newcastle. The house on Bryansford Road is a respectable semi-detached villa just a short walk from Billy's hotel on the seafront. And this is the address that's on my original birth certificate.

THE SCALLYWAG

It's ironic: Billy resisted the partition of Ireland (it almost took his life), but soon after the border had been established, it became his greatest opportunity.

Billy was well known by the police in the south of counties Down and Armagh. He'd trained with many of them when he joined the B-Specials, and his missing arm was a very conspicuous battle-wound that won him hero status and credibility among the police forces. They all knew Billy. Billy was *one of the boys*. Billy could do no wrong.

The border between Northern Ireland and the Irish Free State was eventually agreed by compromise based on religious and political boundaries. This border-by-committee severed some villages, divided townlands, and many farms were left with land on both British and Irish soil. Such a vague and haphazard border was a smuggler's delight.

Billy's opportunities and circumstances changed dramatically with the Second World War.

Billy's first taste of evading the customs checkpoint may have been with his little bus excursions to the Irish market towns, returning home with undeclared goods; it was harmless tax evasion, and everyone who could, did (and still do; wouldn't you?).

As part of the United Kingdom, Northern Ireland went to war in September 1939. The Irish Republic remained neutral. Rationing was introduced in Northern Ireland; but just a short distance across the border there were no restrictions on food and goods.

To understand the situation in wartime Britain, one person's weekly food ration permitted: 113 grams (4oz) of lard or butter; 340 grams (12oz) of sugar; 113 grams (4oz) of bacon; two eggs; 170 grams (6oz) of meat, and; 57 grams (2oz) of tea. Everyone was given a clothing rationing allowance of so many coupons per year. A raincoat required 16 coupons; a jacket, 13 coupons; a shirt, 5 coupons; trousers or skirt, 8 coupons; shoes, 7 coupons; pants and socks, 3 and 2 coupons. By 1943 your clothing ration was just thirty-six coupons per year.

This wartime rationing created a market hungry for contraband goods, and demand multiplied in 1941 with the huge influx of wealthy American soldiers and airmen being stationed in Northern Ireland.

The Royal Ulster Constabulary (RUC) was made a reserved occupation during the war; police officers were forbidden to leave the force to join the wartime services.

The RUC policing duties were extended to include the enforcement of blackout on property and vehicle lights, the protection of post offices and banks, enforcing wartime restrictions on the movement of vehicles, and the rationing of petrol. And *(most significant to this story)* the RUC were given responsibility for the enforcement of Customs and Excise regulations and the collection of revenue.

The war had created a demand, and Billy Adair had the means to satisfy it.

No one was as well connected as Billy. Billy had the means, *and* the unofficial immunity. Billy was the right person, in the right place, at the right time; he had the connections, the resources, and the motivation.

Now, I never knew my father, Billy. I don't want to accuse the man of being a smuggler or a war profiteer, (not directly). However the change in Billy's fortunes from before the war to after the war are remarkable. And what's more remarkable is that no one seems to have questioned his extraordinary change in fortunes.

Billy used to joke about his smuggling during the war: the sausages, cigarettes and sugar, stuffed into pockets, and down his pants. Ha! That's what old women used to do; Billy had the means and the connections to do better than that.

Billy had the means to smuggle on a *wholesale* scale.

It wasn't uncommon for entire herds of cattle and sheep to be moved across the border at night, and a small bribe would make sure that the police officers on duty would be somewhere else and looking the other way at the time of the incident.

During the war Billy was living at Jerrettspass, just one mile from Goraghwood Railway Station.

This quiet stop on the Dublin to Belfast mainline happened to be the official Customs and Excise search point for cross-border trains returning north from the Irish Republic. Coincidentally, and *very* conveniently, his boyhood friend and neighbour just happened to be the stationmaster at Goraghwood Railway Station *during* the war. This valuable friendship would have allowed the wholesale delivery of smuggled goods to be arranged and received by the wagonload.

If it was in demand in ration-strapped Northern Ireland, Billy could've supplied it for you: alcohol, tobacco, butter, cheese, sugar, meat, eggs, tea, bread, petrol, paraffin oil, candles, bicycle parts, clothing, shoes, jewellery...

Before the Second World War: Billy was a one-armed bus conductor in a small rural bus company that was being squeezed out of business by government regulations and aggressive competitors.

After the Second World War: Billy was living in Kilbodagh House, a substantial property with farmland and stables for his daughter's competition show horses; he also owned another sizeable farm either side of Dromantine House; and he owned a profitable granite quarry.

Again, I'm not stating that Billy *was* a smuggler. I'm just saying that $2 + 2 = 4$

If Billy *was* making a fortune from wartime smuggling, I'm not going to make excuses for his opportunism. I could argue that he was just servicing a demand, and if *he* hadn't supplied the contraband someone else would've done it. Or I could say that as a disabled man, the war was probably his best opportunity to set himself up. If he was my Dad I'm sure I would defend this profiteering, or look the other way, or deny it. But as a man I never knew, I can't think of a reason to support what he did, (other than applaud him for getting away with it).

Billy obviously wasn't fit for war service; even if he hadn't been disabled, he'd have been too old to volunteer anyway. Perhaps Billy saw his wartime service as providing people with what they wanted, and taking the personal risk to get it for them.

Billy was a risk-taker, a rule-bender, and a *chancer*. Was he also a wholesale smuggler? It's very, very likely; my heart says it's a no-brainer, *of course he was*. But like I said, I never met the man, and I've got to be sensitive to the feelings of those who knew him. He certainly didn't inherit his wealth; remember, he was the youngest of thirteen children.

The contrast between Billy and my dad is comical. Perhaps it was the Bailie tradition of cabinetmaking that made Dad so correct and so precise in everything he did. (Measure twice, cut once), Dad planned everything carefully and made sure things were proper and correct before proceeding, (he even took all his clothes off to put on his overalls, just to mow the lawn).

Dad didn't volunteer either for active service during World War Two, but for very different reasons to Billy. Dad was young and fit and eager for the fight, but his father wouldn't allow him to go to war. There was no conscription in Northern Ireland, but thousands of young men and women volunteered for military service (including Dad's three sisters). Dad's wartime service involved a pair of bicycle clips, a whistle, and an Air Raid Patrol helmet. I know this really annoyed Dad, because he told me so. He was the youngest child and only son of a member of parliament, and his father refused to let him join his friends who'd already left for their big wartime adventure. Was Dad spoilt? Sure he was – and he resented it. But I bet he was the best turned-out Air Raid Warden the town ever had.

The end of the war should've meant the end to Billy's smuggling (*if* that's what he'd been up to). He'd set himself up with a big house, a couple of farms and a profitable quarry business. But I've heard rumours from one or two credible sources that indicate Billy's continuing interest in the *laundry* business.

Let me explain,... There are two types of vehicle: road; and off-road. Diesel fuel for road vehicles is taxed much more heavily than diesel fuel for off-road vehicles (such as quarry equipment, and farm vehicles). The tax duty difference is significant, but the only physical difference between the two fuels is the colour. If you remove the red dye from off-road diesel, the police can't tell the difference; you can use it illegally, or sell it on as road diesel and pocket the difference.

As a farm owner and quarry owner, Billy would've known all about the temptation to put red diesel in his delivery lorries; all he had to do was filter out the red dye to save himself a heap of money.

It's not difficult to remove the red dye from off-road diesel fuel. Fortunately for HM Customs and Excise today, they've got super-scientific equipment that can sniff out even the tiniest trace of dye in a road vehicle, even if it was put through a vehicle months ago. Back in Billy's day there was no such device: if the diesel wasn't red it was impossible for the police to prove it was illegal.

Removing the dye from diesel fuel is a traditional craft of the Irish border farmers. They are experts of world-renown. The most recent finds include a diesel plant that laundered 12 million litres of fuel a year, and another laundering 6.5 million litres per year. Between them, these two plants were costing the British government well over £9-million each year in evaded tax revenue. Both these diesel-laundering plants were discovered in the Newry area, close to where Billy Adair [may have] established such an operation sixty-odd years earlier.

From what I've been told, Billy's diesel-laundering plant wasn't something hidden at the back of a garage. Billy's diesel filtration factory filled a livestock shed. It was an industrial operation.

Billy had farms with busy tractors to run, and thirsty equipment to operate at the quarry; there was nothing unusual about buying large quantities of red diesel for these businesses. He could easily have been buying red diesel from his suppliers, filtering it, and selling the laundered diesel by the tanker-load. Hiding a large tank of laundered diesel in the back of a quarry delivery lorry concealed below a dusting of gravel is easy and would have made a perfect cover to transport his laundered diesel to fuel stations countrywide. *If* this was what he was doing, Billy's laundry business would've made him a *fortune.*

To compare Billy to my dad again, they're as different as night and day.

As a matter of principle, Dad would declare a conflict of interest if one of the many committees he sat on or chaired had to make a decision about any business in which he had an interest; it's the correct thing to do, regardless of the personal cost. Whereas it's clear that Billy *used* his influence to make things go his way.

How do I feel about being the son of a rascal, and the adopted son of a man of integrity?

I'm proud that Dad was so widely respected for being an upright and honest man. But at the same time I have a cautious respect for my father. Was Billy dishonest because he was bribing people to let him continue his clandestine activities; or are his bribe-*takers* corrupt for allowing Billy to get away with it? I guess if a one-armed bus conductor did everything honestly he might have struggled to provide for his family. So yes, I do respect Billy. I respect him for his resourcefulness and determination (and for getting away with it), (*if* that's what he was doing).

From the time Billy moved from Ireland to the Isle of Man, he became respectable. The business was legal, everything was legitimate, and (unlike many other hotels on the island) he only had one set of accounts: Billy had retired.

But Billy's retirement probably wasn't entirely voluntary.

By 1969 the minority Roman Catholic population of Northern Ireland had suffered discrimination and repression to breaking point. Catholics had been denied the right to vote unless they were ratepayers (and many of them were low-paid labourers living in rented properties, so they weren't ratepayers); electoral boundaries had been manipulated to guarantee Unionist candidates were elected even in predominately Catholic areas; Catholics suffered blatant job discrimination, and discrimination in the allocation of social housing. And they continued to endure prejudiced and heavy-handed policing.

The flip side is, I suppose, that the Protestant majority in Northern Ireland feared becoming the minority if Ireland was united and governed from Dublin. So discrimination against Catholics (who were generalised as republican sympathisers, or more commonly micks, taiges, and fenians) was a survival tactic against a democratic shift in politics.

In response to this established system that secured British rule in Northern Ireland, a series of Civil Rights marches were held in 1969 to protest against these policies of the British government against Northern Irish Catholics.

This catalyst ignited a lot of repressed mistrust and hatred on both sides, which led to the recent 30 years Troubles.

In 1969 Britain was (unofficially) at war again with the IRA. But the new IRA wasn't the same as the old IRA Billy had known. The IRA had split into two new very passionate guerrilla armies: the Official IRA, and the Provisional IRA. Both these paramilitary organisations needed to raise money to pay for their violent campaigns, and a lot of this money came from smuggling and fuel-laundering.

Billy was sixty-six in 1969. The Troubles were more trouble than they were worth to him. He'd made his money, he'd had his fun; he ended his clandestine operations and moved to the Isle of Man as a respectable businessman.

Billy was always a controlling man, but now that he was taking things easier he relaxed his control, and lost his fortune.

Billy had worked hard to amass a substantial fortune. This was the wealth that he planned to leave behind to secure a comfortable future for his family; but he didn't want to bung it in the bank, Billy wanted to invest his money so it would continue to grow.

He carefully studied the markets to find a good, solid investment for his money. But instead of spreading his risk, he invested heavily in shares of Rolls Royce.

When Rolls Royce shares began to tumble at the start of 1971, Billy refused to sell; he couldn't believe that such an iconic British manufacturer could let him down. But on 4th February Rolls Royce went into receivership, (the only thing that eventually saved the manufacturer from bankruptcy was a financial package from the British government who needed to secure their main supply of aircraft engines for the RAF and Royal Navy).

Billy lost his entire investment in Rolls Royce. Hundreds of thousands of pounds just evaporated. *To put Billy's loss into perspective, just £100,000 in 1971 equates to a little over £1-million today;* Billy had lost *millions* in today's money.

He'd have been completely devastated and extremely angry. His vast fortune, his family's inheritance – gone.

Just twenty-three days after this financial disaster, Billy's wife, whose health had been steadily declining for some months, died of a stroke.

Y'know, discovering my father's background hasn't been something I set out to achieve. Sure, I've been curious, but I still don't recognise the Adair family members as *my family*, so I've no natural inquisitiveness driving me to find out who did what, because I never knew the characters. The reason I investigated Billy's life is because I had snippets of information from here, there and everywhere, but no one had put all the pieces of puzzle together to complete a full story of the man's life.

Billy was remarkable by any standards. Youngest of thirteen children born to a farmer, and disabled aged eighteen. Yet he built himself a very successful business empire that bought financial security and middle-class respectability. Regardless of how Billy achieved his wealth, I can't deny that the man was an extremely successful businessman.

Napoleon Hill's renowned twenty-year study of the psyche of successful businessmen might be a blueprint of Billy's character; and such success is acknowledged to be an aphrodisiac. As a man's success grows, so does his libido. But if you're married to a sixty year-old disabled woman, your libido may not be satisfied at home. Laura's familiarity, her vulnerability (and her close proximity), made her a natural target for Billy's sexual attention. But I guess it could've been anyone, (Laura just happened to be his daughter-in-law).

And that's when I became a twinkle in my father's eye.

Brian Bailie

THE ESTRANGEMENT

Now I've got a delicate problem.

I know I've already suggested that my father was a smuggling profiteering scoundrel, an innuendo which some of his family may hate me for. But now I need to feel my way through a much more sensitive subject: I need to clarify the truth from a lifetime of concealment.

To continue this, I've got to say some difficult things about people who can't give their side of the story – because they're all dead. Do I have the right to do that, even though one is my half-brother, and the other is my father?

Dad taught me to be objective and diplomatic with my words, to understand and be fair to both sides of an argument, so I'll give it a shot and see where it takes me, because it's important to my story.

Déjà vu ? The Adair family was rocked and shocked when a previously unknown half-brother and half-sister got in touch and introduced themselves. The Adair family hadn't the remotest suspicion that any other family existed, and they were completely gobsmacked.

The newfound half-brother explained his story and presented irrefutable proof with birth certificates and photographs; there was absolutely no doubt that he was telling the truth.

But don't look at me.

Unbelievably, this is some other pair of skeletons from another cupboard.

In 1989 a different pair of strange relations contacted the Adair family. These are the children of Laura's estranged husband, Robert Adair.

Robert had left Northern Ireland, settled in England, remarried, and naturally enough he had produced two children by this other wife.

I'd call a man with two wives an optimist; the law calls him a bigamist. Happily for Robert, the law never found out. When the bewildered and bemused Adair family explained that their mother and father were never divorced, their new half-siblings were as surprised as they were.

Robert's *other* children are called Bob and Ann-Marie.

Robert Adair's first son to Laura was also named Robert. Two marriages, and two eldest sons called Robert. What do you make of that? Perhaps naming another son Robert was his attempt to start over without completely breaking from his loyalty to his first family; or had he rejected his first family so completely that he didn't care that he already had a son called Robert? Actually, from what I've been able to ascertain, he resisted the idea of calling his new son Robert, but it was his *new* wife who insisted (and what was he going to say?); after all, his new wife couldn't know about his *other* wife.

Bob and Ann-Marie had a loving and happy childhood; they loved and respected their father, whom they described as kind and generous.

Robert was dying when he told his son about his first marriage to Laura; he explained his background and asked Bob to find his first family. And that's what the big fella did; Bob came to Northern Ireland, made some phone calls and knocked on doors asking for leads.

Then Bob knocked on the door of his half-brother, Rob.

Rob's initial reaction to Bob's story was, (as you'd expect), one of shock and disbelief. But after seeing the proof, Rob calmed down; he and Bob had a good chat, and they parted on good terms with hugs and handshakes (after all, Bob hadn't done anything wrong; it was their father who was the rascal).

Bob returned to Northern Ireland in 1995 for another look around, but before he visited Rob he had made a little tour of the places his father had lived, including the old family farmhouse at Killybodagh where he spoke with his father's old neighbour. When Bob met with Rob and told him where he'd been, Rob flew into a rage, threw Bob out and told him never to come back. Shocked and confused by the sea-change in his half-brother's attitude, Bob returned home to England, and has never been back.

When the Adair family left Newcastle in 1969, Laura's eldest son Rob was left behind to take charge of the Avoca Hotel, (ultimately he was given ownership). He was barely eighteen. Rob didn't want to be a hotel owner, he was bored by it, and he satisfied his boredom with drinking and gambling.

When Laura had left for the Isle of Man, she had to leave the ownership of her old Killybodagh farmhouse in Northern Ireland. The farmhouse belonged to Laura, but to avoid Isle of Man tax, on paper it belonged to her eldest son, Rob.

What had enraged Rob by Bob's casual investigation of the old family farm was that Rob had had to sell his mother's farmhouse to pay off his gambling debt; and this was still a very sensitive subject.

Bob returned to England thinking that he'd never enjoy a relationship with his father's first family, but contact was later made with another of his half-brothers, Frank. The rest of the family have accepted Bob and Ann-Marie as their father's other children, their half-siblings. I don't know if Bob and Ann-Marie have come to terms with the fact that their father's marriage was illegal (but does it really matter?).

So, years before I wrote *my* letter, the Adair family had already been shocked by the fact that their estranged father had produced a half-brother and half-sister for them.

I suppose that Bob and Ann-Marie were a kind of trial-run for the revelations of *my* letter, so that when I exposed their mother's secret it wouldn't be so bad for them.

It didn't work that way. In fact I think it made it worse. It was farcical, like a cheap soap opera.

The accepted story is that by 1959 Laura and Robert Adair were unhappily married. *This much is fact.*

Robert was a heavy drinker, a gambler, a womaniser, and he was violent. Often Laura didn't have enough money to buy food for the family because Robert had spent his pay on alcohol and gambling before he staggered home. Laura struggled to feed her children, but sometimes there wouldn't be enough left over to feed herself, and on at least one occasion Laura was found passed out on the kitchen floor, suffering malnourishment. And her husband beat her. Robert would come home drunk and broke, and beat his wife. *This description, though accepted by many, is heavily exaggerated.*

Despite the fact that Laura's children will unanimously swear to the truth of the previous paragraph, unfortunately it is a gross exaggeration that was fabricated to convince them that their father was unforgivably wicked. *He wasn't.*

Why were his young and impressionable children lied to; why were they told exaggerated tales of their father's womanising, gambling, drunkenness and violence?

Robert was my half-brother, so I expect that he and I share a few common characteristics, yet I have <u>no</u> inclination towards *any* of these vices.

I've listened very carefully to the testimony of people who knew Robert well. Unanimously, Robert is described as a gentle-spoken, and kind-hearted man.

Robert *knew* that his wife was having an affair with his father. This is what Robert had told his best friend the night he left for England. If this is so, (and let's face it, it's not the sort of accusation you make lightly about your own father and your own wife), can anyone blame Robert for immersing himself in alcohol, gambling and loose women as a distraction from the gut-wrenching reality of such a screwed-up situation?

The story that Laura's children believe is that their father returned home late again, drunk again, and their mother accused him of being with another woman again. When Laura confronted him, Robert flew into a drunken rage and beat her mercilessly.

However, the story that is more credible is that Robert knew his wife was having an adulterous affair with his father. Because of this screwed-up situation, Robert had turned to alcohol to pacify his depression and anger. *And one* *evening he just snapped;* he lost his temper. He'd have been too afraid of his father to confront him directly so he chose to confront his wife, and in a complete change of character caused by his drunken rage, he beat Laura unconscious.

Striking a woman is an unforgivable and abhorrent act of a bully. I'm not making excuses for Robert, but he *knew* that his wife was having an adulterous affair with his father. I can't imagine how the man must have been torn apart by this indescribable soul-destroying truth. He couldn't take it any longer, and having lubricated his emotions with alcohol, he exploded into a violent rage against her.

Robert beat Laura ruthlessly.

Robert beat Laura so severely that the scars on her back *never* properly healed; until the day she died Laura suffered those tender scars from the lashings of Robert's belt.

Billy and Muriel loved their daughter-in-law, Laura, (each in their own way, obviously). She was their blue-eyed blonde, and they were outraged by their son's behaviour. Billy made a plan to end Laura's suffering, and to remove his son.

Robert was ordered to make a long-haul delivery of stones from the quarry, and while he was away his brothers helped move Laura's children and belongings from their home at Killybodagh to the safety of Billy's house in Newcastle. When Robert returned from work that day, he came home to an empty house.

Robert's brutality had incensed his parents. Billy and Muriel adored their daughter-in-law, and even though their son's behaviour was out of character, the beating he'd given Laura was unforgivable.

Laura was taken to the safe solitude of a rented house at the top of Shan Slieve Drive, a few hundred yards away from her in-laws' house, where she was put in the care of her close friend and midwife, Betty McKay. The curtains remained closed in that house for weeks on end while the swelling and bruising to Laura's face slowly reduced, and the lashes to her back began to heal.

You might be forgiven for thinking that Billy designed the whole conspiracy against his eldest son, Robert. That's certainly how it appears. It appears that Billy manipulated everyone to his own advantage, (with hindsight it's not impossible to imagine that Billy may have planned his son's engagement to Laura, and manipulated their separation to allow him an unhindered adulterous relationship).

I'm positive that Robert's mother had no idea that her husband was having adulterous relations with Laura. And Laura's children were obviously to young to realise what had been going on.

Billy had to make sure that the truth never came out – he *had* to get rid of Robert forever.

To make sure that Robert would forever remain unforgiven, to ensure that Robert would never be able to return to explain the circumstances of his wife's adultery, Billy had to make sure that his son was despised. Robert had to be so vehemently hated by his family that they would never want to see him or talk to him, ever again.

Sure enough, Robert went looking for his family.

He arrived at his parents' house in Newcastle hoping to speak with Laura, and take her and his children home with him.

Billy confronted Robert and offered him a choice: either he stops his drinking, gambling, and womanising, and starts caring properly for his wife and family; or take £500 and leave the country, never to return. Robert accepted the

£500, and was never seen again. *This is the version his children were convinced to believe as the only truth.*

Laura's children believe that their father left them for £500. What nonsense.

The painful truth is equally dramatic:

Billy had to get rid of Robert. Robert knew about his affair with Laura. If Robert exposed this adulterous relationship Billy's reputation would be destroyed, his high status in the Freemasons would be jeopardised, his position within the Orange Institution would be removed; his hard-earned respectability would be in tatters.

Billy made a clear and direct threat to his eldest son.

Billy told Robert to get out of Ireland and never return.

Billy's actual words were: "Get out of Ireland. If you don't get out I'll have you fucking shot."

Robert knew that his father's threat was deadly serious.

He left.

Robert *never* saw his family again.

Laura slowly recovered and settled into her new life with her in-laws in Newcastle.

In 1962 Billy bought the Avoca Hotel on Newcastle's seafront, and Laura took on an active part helping to run this new enterprise.

When Laura's children became old enough, Billy arranged boarding places for them in preparatory schools in Armagh and Dundalk. The children say that they were sent away to school so that their father couldn't find them if he ever returned, but it's more likely that the last thing Billy wanted at his age (and now that he had a disabled wife to look after) was a bunch of young kids thumping through his house; and their absence freed their mother to help him manage the Avoca Hotel.

Did Muriel suspect that her husband was having an affair with the woman they'd just brought into their home? At the time, I'm sure Muriel didn't suspect anything; but later, I'm not so sure. Much later on, there's a whisper of a suspicion that Muriel knew about their affair; but she wasn't in a position to object. Perhaps she encouraged their relationship, realising that Billy needed a woman, and Laura needed a man. Who knows?

I've heard rumours.

I've heard people suggest that one or more of Laura's first six children are my full sibling. I know why they might *think* this, and I appreciate their argument, but I don't fully believe it.

Frank, the youngest of Laura's children with her husband, was born in August 1960, so obviously the thought has crossed his mind that he may be the first of Laura's children with Billy. It's only because Hilary and I have come out of the woodwork and identified this adultery between his mother and grandfather around the time of Frank's conception that he has become confused and has been searching for answers.

If I were to make an educated guess, I'd have to say that in my opinion this giant softy is more than likely my full brother. Does it make a difference to me? No: Frank is still someone I'm getting to know; whether he is 100% sibling, or 75% like all the others, doesn't make a whole lot of difference to our friendship, (but he might come in handy if I need a kidney).

Would it make a difference to Frank to know that he and I share the same parentage? Sure, big time. If Frank was conceived by his grandfather, then he will feel like his conception was the catalyst that broke apart his parents' marriage. And I'm sure it confuses his relationship of trust with his mother, and possibly feels that he has been deceived his whole life. Frank needs to ask his mother for the truth, and I think that he has considered using a spiritual medium to do so.

Would I take a blood test to prove that I *am* a full sibling of any of Laura's first six children? Would it change anything? Hilary and I would still be the ones who were given up for adoption, alienated. I think that a blood test could be opening a can of worms, but yes, I'd agree to a test if it stopped Frank from getting involved with those unholy spiritualists – but for no other reason.

The family sent me a bunch of old photographs.

There is no denying that I look very similar to Billy. He's my natural father after all.

Among the old pictures is a group photograph that shows them all standing in the garden of 39 Bryansford Road. It's shows the six children with Betty McKay, Billy and Muriel, and Laura.

It's dated 1963. The trees in the background are in full leaf, so it must be at least June, which means that I'm in Laura's belly, just three months to go before my birth day.

I guess a photograph is a snapshot of a moment in time that we want to, or need to remember. We take family pictures to show to others, and to keep for ourselves to remember a certain time or event.

When my Claire gave birth to our first child we thought it would be nice to have a photograph of all the mummies on Claire's side of the family. Our little son, Blair sat on his mummy's knee, his grandmother sat next to them, his great-grandmother standing to one side, and his great-great-grandmother standing to the other side. It's a special picture. Five generations of the same family. It's a snapshot of a moment in time when Claire's family was in good health and celebrating a new generation.

This 1963 photograph of the Adair group posing in the garden of Billy's house in Newcastle was a celebration of a perfect moment in Billy's life. I reckon that Billy arranged this photograph because he wanted to celebrate a moment in time when he was especially happy: life was good; he was surrounded by grandchildren who adored him, a wife he loved, and a daughter-in-law he was very actively in love with. And I reckon Billy knew that things were about to change dramatically.

Billy and Laura would've known, for sure, that they were expecting a child together at the time of this photograph. He would've known that these happiest days were numbered by the time-bomb of my gestation. In another couple of months from the time of this photograph, difficult decisions would need to be made about the future of their newborn baby son.

THE ARRANGEMENT

When I met my other family for the first time, the one thing they kept saying to me was that their mother and grandfather loved children too much to just give up a child to adoption. They said that Billy choose my adoptive parents and arranged my placement.

I disagreed with this idea.

Mum had always told me that when she walked into the hospital nursery to choose a baby, she immediately knew that I was meant for her. I was a big, fat, smiling baby, and she just fell in love with me instantly. This is what I truly believed, because Mum had always told me so.

But Hilary argued that when she was a teenager she found a book about adoption in Mum's room, and leafing through it she read how important it is for an adopting mother to tell the child *exactly* what Mum had always told me, almost word for word. Hilary had planted a seed of doubt in the fertile confusion of my mind. But Mum would *never* lie (maybe harmless little white lies, but not a bare-faced lie like that). Did Mum allow me to believe more than she was telling me?

I determined to prove myself right, and that my other family and Hilary were wrong. How could Billy possibly arrange my adoption to Dad? It just didn't make any sense. There's no way Dad knew Billy, they're as different as oil and water.

Everything that I've learnt about Billy describes a determined, analytical, well-connected and very controlling man; but I've also described a man who always put family first.

I found it difficult to believe that Billy could've arranged my adoption to Dad directly. But I accepted that a well-connected and conniving man intent on guaranteeing the very best opportunity for his illegitimate infant, *could* find a way to achieve this goal.

But *how?*

I looked on the map to locate the family home of Billy Adair in Ballylough, near Castlewellan.

Ballylough is the adjacent townland to Annsborough.

Mmm....

A little light began to glow deep in my memory.

Years and years ago, I was at a reception somewhere and I'd overheard a close friend of Dad's, Stewart McCracken, chatting to someone about where his family came from, and he mentioned *Annsborough*. This had always stuck in my head because Stewart and his brother both became very successful city gents; but Annsborough is a humble rural community that sits below a big old abandoned linen mill, it's really not the sort of background I'd expected two brothers to rise from to become such successful city businessmen. Annsborough, even when Stewart was a boy, is the sort of place where kids walked across the fields to school in their bare feet, (the only effective way to warm their feet on a cold day was to find a recently produced clap of dung, and stand in it, which is something I struggle to imagine Stewart ever doing). So because of this dramatic rise in fortunes, Stewart's origin had always stuck in my head.

Could there be some coincidental relationship between Stewart's family in Annsborough, and the Adair family in Ballylough?

I checked the 1911 Census of Ireland for the Castlewellan area to compare the return for the Adair family to the return for the McCracken family.

There's not a shadow of a doubt that Stewart's grandfather knew Billy's father.

- The 1911 census clearly states that Stewart's grandfather was a farmer in the townland of Annsborough. The census clearly states that Billy's father was a farmer on the adjacent townland of Ballylough. They were both farmers, and they lived perhaps less than a mile apart, (in rural parts this is *next-door*).

- Both families were Presbyterians. So both families would have attended the same little Presbyterian Church together every Sunday.

- The age difference between Stewart's grandfather and Billy's father was just two years, (they probably knew each other from school, and were lifelong friends).

- Consequently, they both produced children of a similar age who also grew up knowing each other, going to church together, and attending the same little country school at Annsborough

- Stewart's father and Billy <u>definitely</u> knew each other as long-time friends.

In the 1960s, I've no doubt that Billy knew that his friend's son, Stewart, was a young successful solicitor living in Bangor, County Down. And I'm sure that Billy knew that Stewart and his wife were close friends of Mum and Dad.

Dad had known Stewart long before I was born; and Stewart had married Marie, who was one of Mum's closest childhood friends in Bangor.

Why would Billy Adair target Dad for my adoption?

Well, if Billy was looking for a well-respected family, a loving home, and parents who could offer the best opportunities for his child, Mum and Dad ticked all the boxes. *And* it was no secret that Mum and Dad had been unable to produce children of their own, and had already adopted a son in 1960.

Would Billy Adair have known Dad's father, Tom Bailie? If he didn't know Dad's father, he'd have known *of* him, for sure. Tom Bailie was a well-known entrepreneur and politician.

Dad's father began his career as a cabinetmaker, just as his father, grandfather, and great-grandfather. But the shortage of hardwood and drop in demand due to the outbreak of war in 1914 meant that there wasn't a profitable demand for bespoke furniture. So Tom Bailie became an entrepreneur: he became a cinema owner; he owned a theatre; he owned and operated a tour bus company; he built and owned a hotel; and he developed a successful house agency business, (the business that Dad took over).

Tom Bailie served on North Down Borough Council for 30 years as Councillor, Alderman, Mayor, and was made Honorary Burgess of the Borough in 1953. He was elected to the Northern Ireland Parliament in 1941 (succeeding the late James Craig, 1st Viscount Craigavon) until he was defeated in 1953 elections (after leaving the Ulster Unionist Party mid-term to serve as an independent) by (later to be my mentor) Dr Bob Nixon (who had stood against Tom Bailie as the new Ulster Unionist Party candidate). During his time in parliament Tom Bailie had been elected Chairman of the Ways and Means Committee, and Speaker of the House of Commons.

So there's a good chance that Billy Adair would've known Tom Bailie through their mutual interests in the bus and hotel business (albeit in towns 40 miles apart). But Tom's positions in government would've *guaranteed* that Billy knew about him.

Billy's contacts in the police, Freemasons and Orange Institution could have informed him that Tom

Bailie's only son had been married several years without producing children of his own, and that he had already adopted a son in 1960.

So, if my father had set his sights on having his illegitimate child adopted by Tom Bailie's son, how would he do it, (because Tom Bailie died six years before I was conceived) ?

Billy targeted Dad for my adoption. And he used his lifelong friendship with Stewart's father to make it happen.

I wrote to Stewart, asking if he knew anything about my adoption. He phoned, very surprised at our connection, but stated that he knew nothing about it. However he did agree that his father and Billy went to the same school as each other, and worshiped at the same church together, and both came from adjacent farming families.

But I discovered that Stewart's father and Billy had more, *much more*, in common:

Stewart's father had been Stationmaster at Goraghwood Railway Station while Billy lived just one mile away at Jerrettspass. The Goraghwood Railway Station was the official Customs and Excise search point for cross-border trains on the main Dublin to Belfast line, and Stewart's father was the stationmaster there during the war years while Billy *may have been* smuggling contraband. Stewart even remembers living directly across the road from Goraghwood Quarry, which Billy owned and operated at that time.

And to cap it all, if that wasn't coincidence enough, Stewart's Aunt Flora had owned the Avoca Hotel in Newcastle.

Stewart's Aunt Flora sold the Avoca Hotel to Billy Adair in 1962.

It is no coincidence that Billy Adair targeted my dad to secure my adoption. Like everything he did, Billy planned my adoption with Mum and Dad, and he used his friendship with Stewart's dad to set up the whole thing.

Billy Adair made an appointment to visit Dad at his Main Street offices in Bangor. He introduced himself as a friend of the McCracken family, and explained his background in the bus business (like Tom Bailie), and in the hotel business (like Tom Bailie); and he offered character references from his Bangorian friends in the Freemasons, and the Orange Institution. Dad was never a member of either of these organisations, but Bangor was a small town and Dad would've recognised the names Billy offered as referees, (Billy would've made sure of this). And then, Billy offered his illegitimate son to Dad.

Mum always cried on Hilary's birthday because she felt so sorry that her natural mother was missing seeing her beautiful daughter growing up. And Hilary cried on her birthday because she couldn't understand how her natural mother could give her away. (I don't remember anyone crying on my birthday.)

About eighteen years ago Hilary arrived at Mum and Dad's house in tears. Hilary explained that she needed to find out about her birth-family. Mum threw her arms around Hilary and they both cried; Dad moved into the background and remained silent. I believe that Dad knew too much, and he was avoiding the embarrassment of being asked about something he'd managed to conceal our whole lives.

My adoption to Mum and Dad was formalised at Belfast High Court in May 1964.

We all went: Mum and Dad, Paul and me, and Mum's close friend, Noreen. Noreen is the mother of the twin boys and girl next door, and she had come along to sit with Paul and me while Mum and Dad went into the judge's chambers to sign the adoption papers.

While Noreen was minding us, she was convinced that she saw Mum walk alone across the lobby and leave the building.

In chambers, the judge stood up in surprise as Mum entered, mistakenly thinking that our mother had returned to change her mind.

Noreen was Mum's next-door neighbour; and the judge had just completed the adoption business with Laura. Amazingly, Mum and Laura were almost indistinguishable from one another.

Could Laura have kept Hilary and me?

I've a feeling that *she* could have kept us; but Billy couldn't.

Laura had already suffered and survived her previous humiliations of being jilted by her fiancée for his pregnant lover, and being married to a husband who had nearly killed her; she'd become too thick-skinned to let small-town gossipmongers shame her.

In my best interests, Billy used his gift of persuasion to convince Laura that their baby should be adopted. He knew the importance of a father in a child's development, and at sixty years old he knew it was impossible for him to be there for me in my formative years. Laura reluctantly agreed to the adoption under the condition that it was to be arranged with the best possible family.

Laura's children told me that they had known about a baby brother named James, but she had always told them James had been *lost* at six months. Because there was no grave, they had naturally assumed that their mother had meant that baby James had been stillborn when she was six-months pregnant; they never imagined that she was concealing the truth that James had been *lost* to adoption when he was six months old – she had allowed them believe that I was dead.

Something that keeps niggling at me is a question that you're going to raise an eyebrow at. But now that I've an understanding of the personalities of my mother and father, I wonder if Hilary was planned? Is it crazy to suggest that they wanted me to have a sibling to grow up with? Their story is so strange that anything is possible, *anything is possible.* I know it would please Hilary to believe she wasn't a mistake (like I obviously am); that she was a gift for me, for us to grow up together. It's not inconceivable.

I've been searching my distant memory to recall a man with one arm who visited our house when I was wee. The memory sticks in my mind because he was the first person I'd ever met with a missing limb. I remember a dark brown pinstripe suit concealing a stump where his arm should've been. I don't remember anything else, not even a face. I was very young; Hilary and I snuck into the lounge, said hello, and ran out again. Was that our birth-father? Or is this wishful thinking? (Maybe Paul can remember this visitor.)

Billy and Laura made the correct decision to have me adopted.

When I first learnt about Laura's life I was very sad for her. Her heart and soul were shattered when her fiancée got his other lover pregnant; Laura married and had six children in quick succession; her husband had been violent towards her; she was in an impossible relationship with her father-in-law. And then to top it all, she'd had to give up two children for adoption.

Laura's life wasn't just sad; it was a tragedy. I feel like my father had all the good luck, and my mother had all the bad luck, (if you believe in luck).

Laura deserved more happiness in her life.

Brian Bailie

THE MEETINGS

I knew that I could never meet either of my natural parents. Billy had died in July 1974, and Laura died in February 2010.

Anyway, I think that meeting them would've been very difficult; more for them than for me because I'd unearthed their secret, and that might've uncorked too much bottled-up guilt or remorse or shame (the shock or shame might've killed them). I don't like to embarrass people (actually I do, but not that way), I couldn't have confronted them with my reappearance; meeting them might have been too awkward, I think.

"What was it like to meet your family for the first time?" This is the first thing people ask me.

When I was a kid I was given a Sunday-school prize of a book about David Livingstone. I'd already seen the old movie *Stanley and Livingstone* starring Spencer Tracy as the intrepid Stanley (a Welsh-born explorer and overseas correspondent for the New York Herald) who searched to find Dr. Livingstone (a medical missionary and geographical explorer who'd been lost from the outside world for over six years since he'd taken off into the African jungles to discover the source of the Nile).

I'm sure the book was better than the movie, but I never read it. I loved the book because there was an illustration on the front cover showing Stanley's eventual encounter with Livingstone in 1871, after a seven-month search through uncharted Africa. The illustration appears to show Livingstone surprised by the search party; while Stanley appears elated with his discovery, his hand outstretched in welcome, supposedly exclaiming, *"Dr. Livingstone, I presume?"*

I'd stare at the cover of this paperback book and wonder what it would be like to meet my birth-family for the first time. Would it be equally dramatic? Would I need to mount an expedition into darkest Africa?

Of the six children Laura had with her husband, five survived for me to meet. Robert, the eldest, had died in 2005, leaving Heather, Olivia, Graham, Ewan, and Frank.

By blood they're more than just half-siblings. I'm their half-brother *and* I'm their half-uncle. I'm their Broncle. We're more than three-quarter-relations; we're probably close enough to swap body parts.

I met Olivia and Frank first.

They sailed the Isle of Man Steam Packet to Belfast, and drove straight to Hilary's house in Bangor. I wasn't there, but I've seen the photographs. They were so excited to find the correct address that Frank took a picture of Olivia standing beside the wheelie-bin with Hilary's house number painted on it (like a kid posing beside the gates to Buckingham Palace), they were piddling themselves with excitement, giddy with apprehension.

In the photographs they're all very emotional and very happy, and clearly a little awkward.

They had a meal with Hilary before leaving to travel down the Ards Peninsula to find me. But their Sat-Nav got them lost on the unlit country lanes. I gradually guided them towards me by phone until I eventually saw their headlights bouncing towards me up my long lumpy lane. *Now* I felt awkward. How do you welcome strange relations?

They parked in the darkness away from the light of my door, close to the bracken hedge that conceals a little cluster of beehives. Normally I'd go out and meet my visitors on the path, but it was so dark we would've been bumping into each other and I wanted to see them clearly for the first time; so I leaned out over my half-door, apprehensively gazing into the darkness.

Stanley and Livingstone? *Nope.* But it was lovely; it was lovely and comfortable.

I met Frank with a long, firm two-hand handshake and we stared into each other's face for the first time, each searching for a glimmer of something recognisable in each other. He was stooping, and I was looking up; I'm about six-foot two inches high so I don't get to look up at people too often, but I don't think Frank has ever had to look up at anyone because he's six-foot eight inches; big, like an apprentice giant. Like most big people I know, I recognised Frank as a sensitive big fella; we clicked immediately.

I hugged Olivia long and tight. Our hug felt just right; snug, like a favourite overcoat. So I hugged her again. It felt perfect, (and she stopped talking when I hugged her).

She was effervescent with excitement, and wore a huge grin that made her whole face shine with happiness.

I recognised something familiar in Olivia, yet she didn't look like me or Hilary; then it twigged: she looked like my mum – not my mother Laura, buy my mum, Mum. I remembered Noreen saying that both she and the judge at my adoption couldn't tell the difference between Mum and my mother that day forty-six years ago; so it's not unreasonable that my mother's daughter might look like someone my mother looked like.

It's strange, meeting a completely new person and feeling so familiar in their company, like you've been friends forever. Had I convinced myself that I belonged with these friendly strangers; or was there an instinctive realisation that we belonged together?

Despite our initial connection, we got off to a really bad start.

Frank and Olivia had stayed so long with Hilary that by the time they arrived with me it was late in the evening and nearly time for them to leave. They were booked to stay at their old family hotel, the Avoca, in Newcastle, which was just 50 minutes away if they took the last ferry crossing from Portaferry to Strangford, (or a two-hour journey if they missed the boat). I wanted them to stay longer, of course I did, but I'm well aware of what a drag it is to miss the ferry and have to make that long twisty detour all the way round the top of Strangford Lough; so I encouraged them to catch the last ferry crossing.

I kicked myself for being so flipp'n sensible and for forcing such an awkward anticlimax on their day. But I knew that they'd been travelling since about 5am, and adding a long detour to a night-time journey wouldn't have been fair on them.

I drove ahead to make sure they didn't get lost on the way. The ferry was waiting to make the final crossing when Frank slowed down to thank me and say goodnight before driving down the slipway and onto the ferry.

There was no one about; the little town was asleep; only the hum of the ferry broke the stillness of the damp black night.

I stood at the top of the slipway waiting to wave cheerio. It was 10:46, the ferry should have already departed for the short journey across the narrows to Strangford village; but it didn't move.

I felt like a complete tit.

I'd hustled my newfound brother and sister out of my home, sped them through dark twisty country roads, waved them onto the boat; and they weren't going anywhere. I stood there feeling very uncomfortable, urging, *urging* the boat to go and release me from my awkwardness. Frank, sensing the embarrassment, stepped out of his car to look back at me from the empty deck. We gave each other an awkward little wave, and stood looking at each other, too far apart to speak. All I could think of was the wasted opportunity to be with them, to talk and listen and connect; but they were on the boat, and I was on the slip. It seemed like an age before the ramp rose and the boat disappeared into the darkness.

I phoned Frank the next morning to ask them to meet Claire and me for an early lunch at the Cuan Inn in Strangford village.

This was much better.

Apologising for the anticlimax of the previous evening, we started over again with hugs and handshakes, and this time we were all relaxed, refreshed, and eager to catch up with a lifetime of chat. It was no coincidence that Frank had arranged this visit to coincide with my birthday, and he presented me with a 3kg box of Midget Gems and a kilo of Manx kippers, (ahh,… a true brother's intuition, and worth waiting forty-seven years).

I ordered the Cuan's excellent seafood chowder with a pint of Guinness. "OH! That was your father's favourite drink," Olivia exclaimed with a beam of delight.

Guinness has to be one of the most popular beverages in Ireland; it's hardly a coincidence, (if Billy loved Guinness with the Cuan's excellent seafood chowder, *that* would be interesting); I was being scrutinised for similarities to my half-siblings' grandfather: my soft-spoken conversation, my posture, my expressions, and my choice of drink to accompany my chowder. But what had I expected? I was a close relation whom they'd never met before, and it was natural to try to pick up on little details like this, I suppose.

Olivia began to tell me about brothers and sisters and aunts and uncles and cousins and nephews and nieces, and how shocked and surprised they all were when she'd told them about Hilary and me. I felt like I was failing a memory exam that I hadn't revised for; the names meant nothing to me, just a bunch of faceless strangers, and I struggled to appear interested.

Olivia is the family chronicler: she's the one who hoards boxes of old family photographs and can name each distant face; she treasures the old family birth, marriage, and death certificates; and she keeps in regular contact with the aunts and uncles and cousins here and abroad.

Giddy and gay, ever effervescent, so full of fun and love, Olivia reminds me of Mum so, so much; maybe that's why I fell for her so quickly.

I really miss Mum; she would've loved this *other* family, and they would've loved her, but I'll probably never invite them to meet Mum (Alzheimer's has almost completely removed her mind; she's just a pathetic shadow of herself now). It's not fair, because I know Mum would've been so extremely excited for us all.

Frank is a doer. Frank is the one who bit the bullet and made a plan to come to meet Hilary and me, and he'd arranged it to coincide with my birthday. He's thoughtful that way, and almost apologetic, as if he shares some of the blame for my adoption.

I've spent a long time puzzling all the pieces of my background into a single timeline of events to try to make sense of it all; and I think if Frank does the same it'll help him come to terms with the confusion I think he's trying to understand. If anyone is desperate for answers, it's not me (I'm just curious), I think it's Frank, because he's unsure if his father is Robert or Billy. He has such a good heart. But I think that the appearance of Bob and Ann-Marie, and then Hilary and me, has been much more upsetting for him than he'll ever admit. It's natural to repress upset and confusion, it's normal to want answers, but I think Frank is nervous about what he'll discover, (but hey, the worst thing that he could possibly discover is that he and I are full brothers; does it really matter, and would it really be so bad?).

Frank is the youngest of my part-siblings, but he has been key to keeping the family together; he has tried to accept the facts at face value. Frank was the youngest of the original Adair family, but after all the skeletons were exposed he became a middle child; but in reality he's the big brother, he's the one keeping the extending family together.

I met Graham next.

He was living in Bournemouth. All of my mother's other surviving children remained on the Isle of Man.

Graham was suffering lung cancer and hadn't been given much hope of seeing another year. Is this why I'd decided to go meet Graham first? Probably. I had to fly to England to settle my son into university in Wrexham, so I was already halfway to Bournemouth and I just made the long detour south to meet him.

I'd booked a nearby B&B, memorised the map, and within 10 minutes of arriving at Bournemouth Bus and Rail Station I was knocking on Graham's door.

Livingstone and Stanley? Ummm…no.

Don't get me wrong, it *was* friendly and felt very natural. But it wasn't dramatic. *Comfortable* is the word I've used to describe my first encounters with my *other* family; very comfortable and very familiar, like we've known each other forever.

The door to his apartment was round the side of a house, and the front door opened unto a steep set of stairs. A short "hello" and a handshake, then I followed him up the stairs into a little apartment that reminded me of Mum's cluttered house before she was diagnosed with dementia – boxes and books and DVDs and newspapers, and *everything* piled about the place. I moved some clutter aside to give myself room to perch on the old worn sofa opposite him.

We chatted while candidly studying each other for likenesses. It was really weird; we were like brothers, not by appearance, but likes and dislikes, and the trouble we'd got up to when we were younger – except, I think I'd grown up and he hadn't, (and I'd never been caught for any of the trouble I'd got up to). There was something very soft and gentle about Graham, and his cancer-weakened voice exaggerated this softness.

I spent two days with Graham and his young family before we embraced and said our cheerios. We really connected. And he shared my disappointment that we couldn't have done this a long time ago.

There's something very open and honest about people who've come to terms with the reality of death. I'm sure that's the reason why Graham didn't hesitate to phone me when he heard that he had a surprise half-brother and half-sister. Why wait? Life is short, so live it.

I've got a problem with terminally ill people (and you're going to think I'm a real sicko), but dying really interests me; it intrigues me because the person who is dying often has had the realisation of what's important in life, and what's not. They express themselves openly, and fully appreciate the little things that people just take for granted. *And* they realise the importance of kindness: love for their family, love for their friends, and love and empathy for *everyone*. They love to live, and live to love; <u>kindness</u> is the secret to happiness. And they know that hearses don't have tow-bars: you can't take anything with you, but you *can* leave something beautiful behind.

Spiritually and mentally I'm prepared for death, I'm just not sure I'm ready for the dying bit; it all depends how, doesn't it?

About three years before I met him, Graham had been given only a few months to live. So he'd already been through the whole mental preparation, and sorted things out as best he could for his partner and young daughters for when his time eventually came to leave them. When I first met him he'd been given another, bleaker prognosis; this time he wasn't expected to ride it through.

To be sure, the overwhelming emotion Graham and I shared was an annoyance that we hadn't known each other much, much earlier. He thought that if Hilary had exposed our mother's secret when she'd originally made contact fifteen years previously, it would just have been a storm in a teacup (or a spark in a firework factory). Graham resented that his mother had denied us the privilege of knowing each other, that she had cheated us of our natural entitlement to be brothers.

I liked Graham. I liked him a lot. He was naughty but nice. Mischievous.

The family called him the black sheep. I was warned not to believe everything he told me, (because his family didn't believe everything he told them). Graham said that he just saw things from a different perspective to the rest of the family, and that's how he could remember things that surprise the others.

Graham enjoyed the gentle wisdom that comes from having seen too much of the darker side of life. He was a man of surprising principle, considering where he may have been and what he may have got up to. However, Graham's principles often seemed to conflict with the socially accepted principles of the rest of the world. That's not always a bad thing, (what's that old American saying, *"You all laugh at me because I'm different; I laugh at you because you're all the same"*). He described himself as the fall-guy: if there was trouble when they were kids, Graham got the blame and subsequent beating. He probably deserved it, (I know I caused a lot of mischief when I was a kid). He ran away from home a couple of times, and shortly after moving to the Isle of Man he became known to the police as a troublemaker.

Graham described how things took a turn for the worse while he was working at a Manx glue factory: Apparently it was Graham's responsibility to lock up in the evenings and set the alarms, but by the time he returned to the office one Friday afternoon, everyone had gone home without giving Graham his pay packet. So he opened the company safe and took out £100 with the intention of sorting things out on Monday morning, (they knew he held the keys, and he'd only taken about a week's wages). However one of the owners had called into the office on Saturday morning, and noticed the money missing from the safe. Graham was arrested. It didn't take a lot of explaining for his employers to realise the misunderstanding, and they dropped charges; however the police (who knew Graham's reputation for attracting trouble) wouldn't drop the charges, and he ended up in prison. He was still a teenager, but the lack of detention places for minors meant that Graham spent most of his sixteen-month sentence in adult prisons in England.

He said that he enjoyed prison (I don't think so). Graham had been sent to boarding school since the age of eight, and he said that the prison system applied a similar system of rules, routines and boundaries. He *said* that he just slotted in.

A couple of days before he was due for release, the prison officers ordered Graham to get a haircut. He hadn't had a haircut since he'd been sentenced, so he had big hair like a rock star, but the prison couldn't be seen to allow non-uniform hair, and it had to be cropped, short back and sides. When Graham refused the haircut, three prison officers entered his cell and produced a pair of scissors. The resulting struggle with the scissors caused stab wounds to one of the prison officers, so instead of being released, Graham was put into solitary confinement for six months. All this, the result of a misunderstanding over £100, and a haircut, *apparently*.

He told me that he got involved with the Kray brothers while working as a doorman at a private club. (First you accept a bribe to let them in, then you do them a small favour, and then a bigger favour,…. and before you know it you're up to your neck in their dirty business, and you can't get out.) Reggie and Ronnie Kray had been convicted of murder in 1968 and were serving 30 years imprisonment, but their elder brother Charlie continued to run the firm on the outside, and it was Charlie Kray that Graham *worked* for. I asked Graham what his involvement was with Charlie Kray. With a broad grin he described himself as, "a moral advisor to a henchman".

I know that for a while his work had taken him back and forth from Turkey, returning with undeclared packets of "poppy products". But Graham was just a mule taking the risk for Mr Big.

He told me that he befriended Mary Bell. Mary (dubbed the Tyneside Strangler) had been released from prison in 1980 after serving twelve years for the manslaughter of two young boys when she was ten years old. As you'd expect, she didn't have a lot of friends. If you take time to try to understand Mary you'll discover that she was also a victim, (the illegitimate child of a prostitute who suffered neglect and sexual abuse since the age of four). I think Graham was just attracted to people like that (just as he was attracted to trouble). He had a strange understanding and empathy for people, and he could see past or through the facade to empathise with a damaged and suffering soul.

That sounds strange: a henchman with a heart.

How do I feel about having a half-brother who was mixed up in this kind of dirty business?

He must have thought that I've got MUG written all over me. Graham was so convincing that I couldn't tell what was truth and what was bullshit, but it was all very entertaining. However I had the feeling that Graham fabricated much of his colourful past because the truth of his real life sucked.

Graham *had* led an interesting life, but it was a life without any clear direction that I could identify. He was smart, that's clear; but he never seems to have chosen a mainstream lifestyle.

I asked Graham if he was mentally and spiritually prepared for his death. He explained that during his six-month term in solitary confinement the only book he was given to read was the Bible, and he'd read it at least six times, cover to cover.

I asked him if he understood that Jesus Christ would accept the punishment for all the wrong things he's guilty of; he just needs to ask for His forgiveness. But Graham replied saying that although he realised that he'd done a lot of wrong things, and even though he knew that God loves him, and forgiveness is just a sincere request away, he wasn't accepting the easy way out. "I've done a lot of things I deserve to be punished for; I'm not going to use some last-minute get-out clause to wriggle my way out of it." There speaks a man who has given the subject a lot of thought (or too little), who realises that his life has been less than ideal, but who can't justify being offered a pardon. Is asking forgiveness the same as accepting responsibility and due punishment? Mmmm.

I visited Graham again, four months later, in February 2011. He'd phoned me to say he was feeling very low. It was the anniversary of his mother's death, (*and* her birth – she had died on her birthday); and his drugs were making him feel "like shit". His nurse said she thought he had days to live, the doctor said perhaps weeks.

I arrived with him the next afternoon, and sure enough, even through a cloud of waccy-baccy, he looked like shit. But he was cheerful. His cancer had taken his voice, so he told me in a whisper how really pleased he was to see me.

We had a laugh about the interesting things I'd discovered about his grandfather's past, and we wondered if the family would be upset by any of it. I told him I wanted to write it all down to try to make sense of it, put it into historical context, and figure out the reasons behind the decisions Billy and Laura had made. And he agreed to be my proof-reader; he felt that my parents' story is a remarkable piece of social history, a puzzle that deserves to be put together so we can understand the whole picture. (I just think it's bizarre, but is there such a thing as a normal family?)

If I'd grown up with Graham as my brother, would he have influenced me, or would I have influenced him? I'll never know. It just didn't work out that way. And even though I've only spent a few days in his company, I feel privileged to have known Graham, and love him as a brother.

Hilary and I knew that we'd have to go to the Isle of Man, sometime. That's where our mother and father had eventually settled, it's where they'd been buried; and it's home to our other *other* brothers and sisters.

Hilary had booked to travel alone before Christmas, but just as she was packing her case it began to snow, and it didn't stop snowing until all the airports in the UK had been closed by the heaviest snowfall since the winter of 1962 -'63, (when I was conceived).

Hilary had wanted me to go with her, but I'd kept putting it off. Now she had to plan her visit over again, and she started pleading with me to join her. She was right, of course she was, and I was just making excuses; so I gave in and agreed to go with her in late January.

I'm not sure why I'd been so reluctant to go. I suspected a big Adair party for their extended families to meet their two newly discovered Irish three-quarter siblings. I don't enjoy crowds, and I didn't like the thought of a big party with lots of attention focussed on me from an extensive bunch of relative strangers. Fortunately, Frank had read my thoughts and he phoned to assure me that no such party would be happening.

Frank is a brick. He's the sort of person every family needs. He sees what should be done, and does his best to make it happen, regardless of the inconvenience or expense it costs him: family comes first, even if they're *more* recently uncloseted skeletons. It was Frank who went out of his way to meet and make-up with his half-brother Bob; it was Frank who said he didn't need to see Hilary's correspondence from their mother to prove our parentage; and it was Frank who made the plan to come to Ireland to meet Hilary and me on my birthday.

I'd have gone with Hilary this time anyway, but I travelled more confidently knowing I'd not have to suffer a big family reunion party.

Hilary and I were happy to stay at some convenient B&B on the island, but Ewan wouldn't hear of it. He said that his mother would've wanted us to stay with him, (under the circumstances I wasn't so sure he was right about his mother's hospitality, but we were pleased to accept his generous offer).

Ewan had always lived with his mother, so we were going to be staying in our mother's house.

Ewan politely met us at the door; he was nervous or uncomfortable, or both. Ewan had been the closest to his mother, and it had taken him the longest to accept the fact that she'd kept such a big and closely guarded secret from him. He met us with a polite handshake and spoke 'hello' in the direction of my feet. We were shown through to the old-fashioned sitting room to meet Mac, his wee dog. We perched ourselves on the edge of our seats facing an off TV and an unlit hearth. Little Mac became the focus of our attention and stilted conversation.

Ewan thinks carefully before he speaks, and that's an admirable quality; but... often... it can make him sound like... he's translating... ancient hieroglyphs. I love the careful thought he gives his words; he speaks like a carefully calibrated machine, and can answer a long question with a single well-chosen word, like he's solving a crossword puzzle.

Hilary and I knew that our presence would be especially awkward for Ewan because he'd been so much closer to his mother. Meeting Ewan wasn't disappointing, but it was unremarkable.

Stanley and Livingstone? No; it was more like Stanley meets his next-door neighbour (and his dog).

We were shown into our bedroom. It had been our mother's bedroom, and if I'd read Ewan correctly, it had probably remained unchanged since the day she died. There were twin beds, and Hilary chose to sleep in our mother's bed. It was weird. Our mother had slept here, stared at this ceiling, drawn those curtains; in fact she'd chosen those curtains, and the wallpaper, and the furniture; this room was a reflection of our mother's personality. It was nice, ...but unremarkable.

If our mother had been a ghost, then she should've appeared to us in that room, that night. We didn't expect any apparitions, (and we both slept unusually well).

Frank called with his wife to take us out for a meal and then back to his house to meet his daughters. His youngest daughter burst into tears in the hall, unable to enter the lounge. Eek! Very cautiously Hilary and I stepped out to meet her. It was his daughter's distress that made me realise what Ewan must've experienced when he first met us a few hours earlier: Hilary and I represented the tangible and undeniable proof that Laura had had a love affair with their grandfather that had produced two children whom she had kept a secret their whole life. Up until this moment we'd only been names in a surprise letter, characters in an unbelievable story, names in a tall tale. But now we were standing in her home, and there was no denying our existence, or her grandmother's deception. Everything

Frank's daughter had trusted and understood and loved about her grandmother's character had been shaken into a blizzard of confusion.

I felt upset for her; but was it *my* fault, or was our mother to blame? (With hindsight, I accept the blame for kicking a sleeping dog.)

I met Heather last of all. She lives on the other side of the island from Douglas, on the west-facing shore. If I had a little boat and sailed 30 miles due east out of Strangford Lough, the nearest landfall is the long windswept beach closest to Heather's house, at Kirkmichael.

After a surprisingly long and mountainous drive across the island, we turned in to a long lane lined with big bare winter trees to eventually discover Heather's house at the end of the mile-long trail, overlooking a friendly little glen with a babbling stream.

Stanley and Livingstone? Yes. *Better* than yes.

Encountering Heather was very special. I've described it like love at first sight. I don't know if it was the way she nervously came forward to greet me, or the natural family chemistry, but meeting Heather was like a proper long-awaited reunion. I felt an instant bond. If I'd hugged her any tighter I'd've cracked her ribs. We settled round her crackling hearth to chat, but I couldn't help but keep looking at her. There was a true, almost tangible connection, much moreso than with any of her other siblings (no offence to the other *others*).

When Heather had read my letter six months earlier, she'd become withdrawn. She said she needed to let the news sink in at its own slow pace. I can understand this, and perhaps it's healthier this way than how Frank reacted with shocked acceptance of the facts.

I felt like I'd known all of my part-siblings forever, but the strange magnetism I felt towards Heather is unexplainable. Heather was the eldest of Laura's daughters, and she told me that she vaguely remembers being told to look after a baby in her aunt's house sometime about 1963. If I really was that baby, could that brief encounter so long ago have created such an instinctive bond? If so, I wonder what I would've felt had I met my mother; could it have been as magical? (For a lot of reasons, I doubt it.)

Heather lived in a remote little house nestled within the protection of tall bare trees, and embraced by the contours of the sweeping hillside. It was very similar to the wee house that I lived in when I was farming. Everything felt just right for me: the place, the homeliness, and Heather's magical welcome. Is *that* why I connected with her so well? No: I believe there *was* a magic of sorts, something I can't explain, (something I'm looking forward to again).

I don't know how she felt about meeting me. (Probably glad to see the back of this Irish weirdo.)

On a grey and blustery Sunday morning Hilary and I walked up the hill to Douglas Cemetery to visit the family plot.

Hilary said she needed to see it, but I was indifferent; to me a grave is a just a bunch of buried bones, the person has gone, (but I know that Hilary sees things differently, I know she still visits our granny's grave, and Dad's nearby). There was very little written on the headstones, just their name, age, and the date they died. In Ulster it's common to see old headstones with lots of information about who and when and where, and maybe a little Biblical prose underneath; these Adair inscriptions struck me as impersonal and abbreviated, (like a war grave).

It's a wide family plot, originally purchased as a single grave when Billy's wife died, and then Billy was buried in the adjacent plot; so the family had a little polished granite boundary erected around the two to make it one big family grave.

Billy is buried with his wife lying on one side of him, and Laura, his lover, on the other side. *The old scallywag.*

Frank dropped us off at the little airport, and we said our cheerios.

We checked in and I walked on ahead of Hilary to the waiting area upstairs. I looked up and saw Heather sitting there, just staring down the stairs patiently waiting. It was a delightful surprise (and that thing happened again where so much is said without saying a word). When Hilary appeared, Heather produced a little worn box and insisted that Hilary accept it. Inside was a fine gold wristwatch that had belonged to her mother. I was overjoyed for Hilary; at last she had something tangible, something special and personal that had belonged to her mother; a physical connection to the person who gave her life.

It made me wonder how I'd feel about being given something that had been personal to Billy, my father. I'm not sure I'd like that. I don't think I need a tangible connection.

I also have bunch of newfound cousins, (what's the collective noun for cousins?).

The first *other* cousin I met was Amy. Hilary and I met with her in Belfast one afternoon, and she was lovely. We spent about two hours listening to Amy while we balanced on stools around a very high cocktail table in Café Vaudeville. She was full of stories about our mother and father, and produced photograph after photograph of our parents. It was refreshing to hear the more objective point of view of our existence. The pictures Amy showed us of our father were just pictures of an old man in his late sixties; but she produced several pictures of our mother, Laura. She was a beautiful young woman: a tall and lean, fair haired, blue-eyed woman with a smile that would sell toothpaste.

After meeting Amy it was an easy decision to agree to meet the other cousins. Four cousins and their accompanying spouses found their way to my house on a sunny spring afternoon in April to meet Hilary and me. Another cousin had decided not to come, and another seemed to get lost and hasn't been seen since. Eight relative strangers were enough anyway.

My home began to fill with friendly strangers and our stilted conversation. Hilary and I knew that we were a great curiosity to these new relations because we are the result of what would've been a family scandal had our mother's secret ever been disclosed while she was alive. All these cousins had known their Aunt Laura very well, and all remembered their Great Uncle Billy. Hilary and I could feel ourselves being scrutinised for family resemblances, just as each of our part-siblings had scrutinised us, but this time there were eight of them including spouses, all at once.

Fortunately my Claire had prepared a tableful of afternoon teas and home-baked treats, so just as the conversation began to falter awkwardly, we were invited to squeeze around the table to eat. This was much better, all bunched up, and the chatter enlivened with the more relaxed atmosphere and the distraction of food. We had a great laugh, (the circumstances of our family connection were hardly mentioned), we were getting to know each other as friends, which was so much easier than trying to get to know each other as cousins. The thing about Ulster is that if any two people don't know each other directly, they'll almost certainly share a mutual acquaintance who connects them either by blood or friendship; so as the teapot was passed about the table, and the butter, jam, and cream lubricated the scones and soda bread, the craic was mighty.

The subject of a couple of anecdotes came around to motorcycles. Motorcycles appear to be an Adair peculiarity. All of the male cousins owed motorcycles, as did my *other* brothers; in fact one of the cousins had raced in the

Isle of Man TT a few times (but I couldn't ask him about this because he was the cousin who'd gotten himself lost on his way to my house). The curious thing is that I also have a motorcycle, (although I much prefer my push-bike). Coincidence perhaps; or are we natural-born risk-taking adrenaline-junkies, born of the breed that coined the phrase "No Surrender". Ha. It's hard to beat the buzz of adrenaline that hits you when you accelerate hard on a motorcycle, or take a corner at speed – but is it an inherent thing, this love of buzz?

Having met my other siblings and a bunch of other cousins, has it helped me connect with my family of origin?

Well sure it has. But I'm still Brian Bailie. I'll never be Jim Adair. It's easier (much, much easier) for the Adair family to accept me as one of theirs, than it is for me to accept that I'm one of them.

They've got a family with two additional half-siblings by their estranged father, Bob and Ann-Marie; and another two three-quarter-siblings by their mother and grandfather, Hilary and me. For them, it's like a surprise inheritance from a distant relation.

I've already got a family and extended family that I grew up knowing and loving, and an established identity and family background that I've known my whole life. It *is* confusing. For an adopted person to adapt to the birth-family, it's not been easy to see how I fit in.

I know they mean well and want to embrace me as a brother, but I don't think they understand that the gap between us is wider from my side, than it is from theirs.

I need a little more time.

Hilary and I were invited to two Adair family events in 2011.

The first occasion was Graham's funeral in Bournemouth. I don't know if they understood why I didn't attend; I'd spent time with Graham when he'd asked for me. He wasn't at the funeral, just his old cold body in a box. Hilary went; she endured quite a long and stressful round-trip for the short funeral service.

And one of Olivia's daughters was married in the summer. I *almost* agreed to attend, but I made my excuses; not because I had a lot of other things happening, but because I still felt like a friend of a friend. A family wedding, with maybe a hundred guests, many of whom I'm related to somehow, it just felt like too much all at once. Hilary was there. I feel a little regret for not attending the wedding because I don't want to appear rude or disinterested, but I think I might have regretted attending it and felt strangely self-conscious.

In a way I feel like I've whooshed into their lives in 2010, and crept out again in 2011. It's not like that; things take time.

I think it's been different for Hilary because this reunion has been her quest since she was a wee girl, and she's embraced our other family wholeheartedly.

I suppose I could compare how I feel to how Heather felt after she had read my letter. She allowed a long time to pass for her to accept the facts, for her to accept that her mother had secretly borne two children and given them away. And that's healthy. Well, I need time to let this situation sink in so that I can make sense of my relationship to my half-brothers-half-nephews and half-sisters-half-nieces. Being a broncle is confusing enough without all the baggage that comes with it.

THE CONNECTIONS

Okay, so I'm Billy's son, and I'm Laura's son; there are bound to be similarities in my personality and appearance that I share with each of them.

Perhaps the most obvious in appearance is my build, and this seems to come from my mother. I'm tall and lean, same as she was. Billy's children were also tall, but more cuddly, perhaps.

Most of the photographs that I'd seen of Billy were of him either as a very young man, or as a senior citizen. There was one of Billy and Laura photographed as a couple on her wedding day to his son; spookily, it appeared a little like Billy and Laura were being wed, (like wishful thinking).

I've seen a picture of Billy as a boy of about 10, and there *is* a strong resemblance to me at that age, but nothing astounding. A lot of his middle-age photographs are poses, nothing relaxed, nothing that allowed his true character to show through. And there are dozens of him as a senior citizen, (the shape of me to come, perhaps?).

Frank visited Northern Ireland with his wife in the summer of 2011 with the intention of mixing a little sightseeing with a couple of family visits. One fine morning we headed north and west on a roundabout trip to meet one of my *other* nieces.

We stopped off at the Giant's Causeway to stretch our legs and dander about the big puzzle of basalt columns, (always worth seeing, but not always worth going to see). Unlike the old days of the Troubles, the place was polluted with tourists hopping from one stepping-stone to the next and taking photographs of each other in various states of exhaustion.

There's a wishing seat, a natural little throne of hex-shaped pillars somewhere among the main headland of columns, but it's difficult to find it; I think you just decide which formation of rock fits you most comfortably, and that's your wishing seat. In a way that's what I was attempting with the Adair family – I was wishing to see how I fitted in to this family puzzle. If I was just the child of Laura, it would be easy; but because Billy is two generations older than me, my relationships with the Adair family is complicated and twisted like no family tree should be.

I wandered off on my own to the end of the causeway where it disappears below the waves in the direction of Scotland. It was a fine clear day; the sea was calmly swishing around the edge of the rocks, which made it difficult to image how destructive this coastline had been to a Spanish Armada a little over 400 years ago. I love the sea, and the deep calm waters tempted me to dive in to their darkness to enjoy the shocking invigoration of the cold, and the clean salty taste of the sea; but skinny-dipping in view of a thousand tourists' cameras wasn't a good idea. Shame. Time to go.

Frank plugged in his Sat-Nav, and we headed off to discover this *other* niece of mine who lived on a farm somewhere on the far side of Lough Neagh. Technology is great, isn't it? The little Sat-Nav must have been programmed for "scenic route only". We ignored the road map and the obvious road signs, and obediently followed the instructions of the authoritative Sat-Nav. The landscape and skyscape were stunning off the beaten track; the roads became twistier and narrower and slower, until at last the

Sat-Nav told us that we had arrived at our destination. We looked around us; we looked at each other; we were lost, but probably within a mile of our destination. Frank phoned for directions, and within a couple of minutes a boy appeared on a quad, waving for us to follow him down a dusty bumpy track to a smart little house perched on the side of the green hill that overlooked an amazing panoramic sweep of Ireland that extended from the undulating Sperrins in the west, to the Mournes in the east.

We had arrived at the home of Gillian, who is the daughter of Billy's son, David. Billy's sons were my half-brothers, so Gillian is my niece. Busy, blustery and straight-talking; it was great to enjoy her fresh and forthright perspective on the relationship between my parents and the circumstances of my secret conception, birth and adoption. She didn't *know* about my existence prior to my letter to the family, *however* she had been aware of rumours. But Gillian wouldn't speak of the rumours, only the facts, and I appreciated that; too often a rumour can become gossip, and gossip can become the accepted facts and offend the innocence of truth; so everything I was told, Gillian told as factual truth, (which left me wondering what the rumours had assumed of the situation).

Obviously Gillian was able to tell me lots about her father, David, my half-brother, and I was shown lots of his photographs. One picture showed him in military uniform, which surprised me; when I questioned how old he would have been she said that he had lied about his age to volunteer for service in WWII aged 15.

Gillian didn't seem to have many photographs to show me of my father; but then she surprised herself by unearthing a photo of Billy taken about 1938, when he would've been maybe 35 years old. I laughed out loud. If ever there was proof that I'm Billy's son, this photograph was it – I was looking at a seventy-three year-old photograph of *me*. The studio photograph shows Billy and his wife seated in a relaxed pose: his head slightly tilted (as I do); asymmetric ears (same as mine); smiling with his eyes, but his left eye noticeably narrower than his right (just as I do); a slightly awkward half-smile (like mine); and a headful of unmanageable hair beaten into submission with a liberal application of Brylcreem (yeah, I know all about unmanageable hair). For the first time I could directly identify with my father, I could almost read his mind in that photograph.

I asked for a copy of my doppelganger, and I sent it to Hilary as soon as I got home. She laughed aloud too, as did my Claire and my kids. It was uncanny.

The name of my father was missing from my birth certificate; the only evidence I'd had to indicate that Billy was my father was the word of a retired social worker, and the missing letters between Hilary and our mother. This was it – this photograph was the undeniable evidence that I needed to satisfy me that Billy (the Winger, the scallywag, the chancer, the loverboy) *was* my father.

People ask me if I feel any connections with places; like déjà vu? I do, but is this instinctive, or a natural magnetism towards undeniably beautiful places? Billy and Laura both grew up under the gaze of the Mourne Mountains. In fact the Mournes passively overshadow my whole story. But the Mournes are so remarkably beautiful from every angle it's difficult *not* to be drawn to them, so I don't know if my love of the Mournes is instinctive or not.

I've driven past Billy's old house on Bryansford Road every time I pass through Newcastle; I have to, that's the way the traffic system takes *everyone*. When I first saw this address on my birth certificate I went looking for it. I was kind of expecting something much more humble because all I knew about my origins was that I had a farming background, and my parents couldn't keep me, so the last thing I expected to see was a very respectable semi-detached villa in a prosperous part of the town. It didn't feel familiar to me because this was most probably where I was conceived; rather it felt familiar to me because it looked like so many houses that I remembered from my youth, growing up in the well-to-do Ballyholme area of Bangor.

When we were very wee our family holidays were either down south in Ireland, or on the Isle of Man. My *other* family believe that we were taken on holidays to the Isle of Man because Dad knew that our birth-family was living there, and this was a means to allow Billy to look at his two little lost children. I don't know; but I doubt it. We usually went to Port Erin in the south-west, and avoided the busyness of Douglas on the east coast. But Hilary has shown the *others* photographs of us in Douglas, and they exclaimed that we were just yards away from Billy's hotel, and it *can't* be a coincidence. But it *could* be.

The Isle of Man is very familiar to me as a near distant horizon. I could see it from the farm I worked near Ballywalter, and the little primary school that my kids went to (and my youngest still attends) sits on the shore at Cloughey directly facing the island.

The island appears so close to the Ards Peninsula, it's truly tantalising. I've considered paddling my old canoe to the island, however it's about 30 miles away, and with the current it's probably another seven or eight miles paddling, which would be about ten hours canoeing, (which would be blistered hands and a very sore arse), so I remain tantalised; although, having said that, this piece of frigid Irish Sea is perhaps a healthy obstacle. I think it would be awkward if we were all living a few miles apart.

There's an odd connection that's just so farcical that my *other* sister Olivia was worried I'd take it as an insult.

Years ago, my mother won a life-size cuddly clown at a funfair. And: she named it *James* (the name she gave me on my birth certificate). She kept this life-sized cuddly clown in her house, and even had a bedroom for it where she tucked it into bed. She wasn't going dotty; she was just having some fun (oh yeah?). So I was gone, but not quite forgotten. (Do I feel a longing to join the circus? Yes, that's it: I'm a closet clown – finally, after all these years I realise my true calling in life – quick Nelly, pack your trunk...)

There's another peculiar little anecdote that I didn't know where else to mention in this story. Graham originally told me about it, but it was so bizarre I naturally thought it was just another of his tall tales, but then his siblings verified his story:

My mother witnessed a bright light in the sky.

She'd been out walking her little dog on a lonely Manx headland, and she returned home with mild shock. And from then on her personality became much happier and carefree. This would've been about 2008.

If you're like me, you're raising an eyebrow right now. But this is what the family tell me. It might have been something supernatural, or it might have been something neurological, or spiritual, but whatever it was it changed her.

And on the subject of the bizarre and questionable, you can join a ghost tour of the Isle of Man, where one of the attractions is the building that used to be the Conister Hotel where the figure of an elderly one-armed gentleman descends through the air where some stairs have been removed, shuffles some papers and returns up the nonexistent stairs again. I visited the Empress Hotel, which now extends to include the old Conister Hotel building, and I asked the receptionist about the one-armed ghost. She told me to get out; she wouldn't even let me stay for lunch. Mmmm.?

Of all the connections I've made, the most amazing (for reasons I cannot understand) has been my initial connection with Heather. I don't know what happened there, but there *was* something spookily, magnetically instinctive.

Having said that, probably the most remarkable connection of this entire story is the very strong possibility that I have discovered a full brother in Frank. If 2+2=4 Frank is a full brother to Hilary and me. But I also accept that in real life 2+2 doesn't always make 4, and I could be quite wrong. Frank and I share similarities, but you'd expect that anyway because if he's not my full brother, he is my three-quarter-brother. Whether he and I are full brothers or not doesn't change *my* story, but I realise that it changes his. I realise that this question of parentage may be a source of a lot of confusion for Frank, and like I said earlier, I'll do the test if it'll help uncover the facts.

But perhaps I'm looking at my situation all wrong. Perhaps, instead of trying to connect with my birth-family as my birth-family, I should put the blood relationship aside and focus on simply developing lasting friendships. They are all people whom I'm more than happy to befriend – I think that I've just confused myself by trying to come to terms with how and why we are related, and *that* really doesn't matter (does it?).

THE STIGMA

I think the biggest stigma for an adopted person is the thought that they've been given away, in the same manner as you might give away unwanted clothes to a charity shop. And their adoption is sort of pot-luck, (you get given to the family you're matched with without any say).

In the 1960s adoption was less complicated than it is today, and I think that's why I'd always believed that Mum *really had* just walked into a nursery full of screaming little illegitimates and instinctively chosen me, like we were made for each other.

The last foster-child I prepared for adoption was matched with a couple in Londonderry, and because the Roman Catholic Church manages adoptions in that area, my little friend's adoption was arranged by nuns. This really worried me, (not because this was a Protestant adoption managed by Roman Catholic nuns), but because I wondered what a bunch of cloistered spinsters would know about creating a family. So it was with a high degree of scepticism that I met the adopting parents to-be, prior to their introduction to my little friend. I gotta hand it to those nuns, that last foster-child of mine, that was a *perfectly* matched adoption. The parents even looked like my little friend, they looked as if they were his natural parents. And when I introduced them to each other, they clicked, instantly – it was a beautiful match, (thank you ladies). That adoption took two years to set up for the parents, and about six months preparation for the child.

Things were a lot different in 1963 to how they are today.

In fact my adoption was a private adoption, which was unusual and quite difficult in the '60s; but for someone as cunning and well-connected as my father, I expect that my adoption was just another of his carefully executed plans. And discovering this fact has reassured me that I wasn't *given up* for adoption, and my placement wasn't a matter of *pot-luck*. Mum always emphasised that we three were *her* children; that we were *meant* for her. And what Mum meant was that she had put her complete faith in God that she would have children; so (after six years of childless marriage) when she was offered a son, (my brother Paul), Mum knew that this was God giving her a child, which He had chosen for her. Mum would always get very upset if we ever suggested that our family was anything other than predetermined.

I don't go looking for adopted people, but they often make themselves known, like they've got a big problem about it, like they're special and deserve sympathy; oh, boo-hoo. Many have major hang-ups, and others don't give the matter a second thought. Generally, adopted children are offered a better chance in life than if they had remained with their natural parents.

Of course it's a status that never goes away. When a doctor asks me if I'm aware of any congenital medical conditions I'm bound to say that I've no idea. I'm certainly not ashamed of being adopted, and Mum and Dad never purposely hid the fact from anyone.

I've already mentioned that Moses and Jesus Christ were both adopted as infants. But it's difficult to relate to people like that. It's easier to relate to adopted people of more recent generations, people like:

* former President of South Africa, Nelson Mandela.
* former US President, Bill Clinton.

* Russian businessman, Roman Abramovich.
* singer songwriter, John Lennon.
* singer songwriter, Debbie Harry.
* actress, Marilyn Monroe.
* entrepreneur and Apple Inc co-founder, Steve Jobs.

Okay, so I'm cherry picking, but look at it this way: it's *highly unlikely* that any of these people would have achieved the success they enjoyed had it not been for their adopted upbringing.

As a foster-father I had to read a lot of guff about *Nature versus Nurture*: your nature is your inborn, inbred instinctive traits; your nurture is the experience of your upbringing and surroundings that moulds these traits. I find this relentless focus of social workers on this nature/nurture argument mind-numbing. It's just common sense.

I am the child of rural people: my father grew up on a farm, and my mother grew up on a farm. But I was raised in the town: Dad was a businessman, son of a businessman; and Mum was a housewife, daughter of a gentleman.

The world that suited my nature was far removed from the world of my nurture. I unenthusiastically attended at a preparatory school and grammar school (until the headmaster told me that it would benefit the both of us if I didn't come back). And I still struggle to identify a career path that feels natural to me.

I took a job as a welder when I was 17. It was while I was working in that factory that I met someone I really connected with. He was also a welder, but he loved the outdoors; he and I would often spend our weekends walking miles over fields exploring and discovering the nature around us. We had ferrets, and often we'd return home laden down with rabbits, pockets full of berries, (both of us jollied along by a little of his home-distilled poteen). I really felt instinctively *right* when I was with him, I felt like the rural lifestyle and this fascination and appreciation for nature was in my blood. (It certainly wasn't in Dad's blood; he refused to eat any meat that hadn't been bought from the butcher.)

I met Claire when I owned a small commercial art business in Bangor. I needed an apprentice for my sign artist, and Claire had replied in response to my advertisement. I liked her, my artist liked her, so we agreed to give her the job. She liked my artist; she hated me. My wee business did okay considering there a recession happening, but I wasn't *that* happy, it wasn't what I wanted to be doing indefinitely. After Claire had left for a career in the civil service we kept in touch, and she grew to like me a bit better, a lot better eventually, and we began to think about getting married. But I didn't want to get married while I was self-employed, it wouldn't have been fair because I'd never have been at home.

So Claire phoned one day to say that she'd found me a job that came with a wee house; and if I liked it, we could get married and I could start work that summer. When I heard it was a job on a farm I didn't hesitate, and we shocked Claire's parents with the news that we were getting engaged and planned to be married within the next six weeks. That's how I became a farmer. The most enjoyable and most fulfilling job I've ever had.

When it became too difficult to remain on the farm I started doing some cabinetmaking, and that led to other things, which eventually took me to China where I established a little manufacturing business, (but that's a whole other story).

The filth and stink and overwhelming populous of industrial China is a galaxy away from Ireland. It's usually late in the evening when my connecting flights return me into the cool clear air of Belfast. Driving home down the Ards Peninsula, we pull over near Saltwater Brig by the calm shores of Strangford Lough for my lungs to expand and rejoice with the icy cleanliness of the night air. Looking to the south, across the dark calm lough waters I can pick out the distant gentle silhouette of the Mournes, reassuring me that I'm home again. *This* is where I belong, in the countryside by waters and familiar mountains, (not in that assault on the senses that is east coast China; sorry partners).

On the subject of China, I know that there are many Western parents who have adopted a Chinese infant. This is a touchy subject, but I have a little experience in China, and I feel that people must realise that not all these Chinese babies have been willingly offered for adoption by their true parents. If a Chinese couple produce more children than they are permitted by regional law (typically one child only) their additional babies are at risk of being forcibly removed by government officials, and it is these government officials who profit directly from the adoption of the child to a well-meaning, naive Western family.

Furthermore, every year there are thousands of infant kidnappings in China, thousands and thousands. Infants are stolen to order for two reasons: Either a wealthy couple have decided to have a child, but (because of the work ethic in China) they have left it too late to reproduce naturally, or they don't want to suffer the inconvenience of a pregnancy, so they buy a child; Or, the infants are stolen and offered for adoption to Western families by persons posing as the real parents. If you think this isn't possible in a modern civilised society, I'm sorry to tell you that China is a whole other planet removed from many of the accepted ways of the West. I'm not saying that all Chinese babies offered for western adoption have been removed by force or kidnap; what I'm saying, is that it's a possibility, and something that you must investigate properly (regardless of how honest and sincere the Chinese adoption agencies appear).

On a lighter note: as a foster-father, I know that being able to explain that I'm adopted has reassured some of the kids whom I've had to prepare for moving on. To compare adoption to an upbringing within the social care system, for me it's a no-brainer; for me it is so important that a child is removed from the interference and mollycoddling of social workers. In my experience that is not a healthy environment for a child to thrive, for so many reasons. A child needs a mum *and* a dad; a child needs unconditional love; a child needs long-term security. A child in care will only receive a compromised version of what they need to thrive, and that is why I have always actively encouraged the idea of adoption when it has been appropriate. Adoption removes a child from the well-meaning interference of social workers; adoption gives a child an identity within a stable family unit, and better opportunities for the rest of their life.

Being adopted doesn't mean you give up being part of one family to become part of another; it means that you're a significant part of both families.

Brian Bailie

THE END...

I don't think there *can* be an end to a story of adoption and reunion.

The break that Mum and Dad caused in the Bailie family tree was grafted with a little complicated shoot of Adair, but the tree remains a Bailie tree.

You're probably wondering how my kids feel about it all, since my story indirectly affects them too.

Hilary married, so her surname changed anyway. But my kids are Bailie kids; both my sons will remain as Bailie. Bailie is our family name and identity.

And perhaps because of this identity and loyalty to the Bailie family name, I will never fully accept that I am an Adair in anything but blood. I expect that I'll always be a little confused about accepting my *other* brothers and sisters as my full relations. I want to get to know them better; they're a great bunch of folk whom I'm pleased to be an other part of. But at the same time, I've really just met them; there's a whole bunch of catching up to do, not about who did what and when, but just to develop friendships.

Is discovering my birth family an insult to Mum and Dad? Is it like Mum and Dad borrowed me to raise me, and now I'm going back to the family of my birth? Of course not; Dad is dead a while now, but I know that he'd have been pleased for us; and if Alzheimer's disease hadn't devastated Mum, she would be enjoying this adventure more than anyone, for sure she would; she'd have been delighted for us, and *so* enthusiastic, she'd have been right in the middle of things…..

I met with Paul this afternoon. He and his wife were passing through London and had made the detour to visit Belfast to touch base with friends and family. The weather was unpredictable so we arranged to rendezvous at the Ulster Museum to chat as we wandered around the exhibits. As we relaxed over drinks and cakes in the café I mentioned in passing that I'd been writing this story of my adoption and the subsequent family reunion. Sipping the froth off a large cappuccino Sharon asked me if my book had a purpose. A purpose? I didn't start out to write a book, my original *purpose* was to help me make sense of the circumstances surrounding my existence, to help me understand where I fit in.

Now that I've created this rambling bunch of thoughts, perhaps my story will serve the purpose helping other adopted people realise that there is no shameful stigma that comes with being adopted; perhaps parents who are considering offering their infant for adoption can realise that adoption offers many opportunities that can only benefit a child far more than the social care system can offer (and your child isn't simply lost forever). And perhaps students of the theories of Nature versus Nurture will appreciate the confusion of this child with a strong natural connection with the countryside, but who was reared as a middle-class townie.

Essentially this has been a journey of discovery for me, a quest to discover who I am and where I'm supposed to fit in. I can't say if telling my tale has helped me as much as I'd hoped it would, but I think it's time I stopped writing.

ABOUT THE AUTHOR

Brian Bailie lives in the green lumpy landscape between the lough and the sea on the Ards Peninsula of Northern Ireland, a world away from his design and manufacturing business in China, which he owns with his Texan partners.

Brian's other books include: Prepare Yourself for China, the visitor's survival guide to China; and, Alzheimer's Timeline, a layman's study of dementia in the family.

www.broncle.com

CPSIA information can be obtained at www.ICGtesting.com
Printed in the USA
BVOW011226040412

286858BV00008B/6/P